Henrietta Lacks

THE UNTOLD STORY

Henrietta Lacks

THE UNTOLD STORY

A MEMOIR BY

RON LACKS

Text Erika Winston

Design Adeline Media and Grade Design

Copyright © Ron Lacks

ISBN 978-1-6596381-7-2

First print January 2020

CONTENTS

1

MY REASON WHY

On April 18, 2017, I woke up and went about my morning routine, just as I do every single day. I took a shower, put on some clothes, and checked on my mother, who I've been caring for since her stroke eight years ago. Baltimore's WJZ is my news station of choice in the morning, so I turned it on to see what Gayle King and crew were going to be talking about on *CBS This Morning*. I had no clue that my family would be the topic discussion that morning.

My name is Ron Lacks. I am the oldest grandson of Henrietta Lacks, a beautiful and strong woman whose cells have become one of the most important cell lines in the history of medicine. My grandmother's story gained public attention in 2010 with the publication of the book *The Immortal Life of Henrietta Lacks* by Rebecca Skloot. Oprah Winfrey bought the rights to the book, and soon after we received our first contract from HBO. I'll go into more detail about that later, but in April 2017, the HBO movie was about to come out. So, it wasn't a complete shock to see Oprah and Gayle discussing my family on that morning. But something about that interview touched my heart deeply, pushing me to write this book.

The beginning of the segment didn't bother me much. I already knew what they were going to say. It had been seven years since the book came out, so I was used to hearing people talk badly about my family. I didn't like it, but I heard it so much that I had built up a shield to it. I knew I would hear the same lies about the poor ignorant Lacks family and how Rebecca Skloot came along and made our lives better. All a bunch of bullshit. But then the conversation took a turn that I wasn't expecting.

First, I listened to this actress go on and on about Rebecca Skloot—the woman who exploited my family for her own gain, leaving us torn and dishonestly portrayed for the entire world to see. The actress called her a "force of nature" and "incredibly smart but incredibly determined." She said that when Rebecca Skloot has her "mind on something, she will get it." I agree with every one of those statements, but not in the way that woman meant any of them. In my opinion, the only thing Rebecca Skloot was determined to do was use our family's pain to sell her books and get rich. I believe her mind was on making money, and she did not stop manipulating my family members until she got what she wanted. Rebecca Skloot's actions pulled my family apart and it made me mad to watch this actress gush over her like some messiah come to save the poor black people.

Then came the comment that really moved me into action. Speaking about my Aunt Deborah (we call her Dale), Gayle King says with a laugh, "Deborah was a little crazy." *What in the hell did she just say? Did she just call my aunt crazy?* I could hardly even listen to anything after that. I just kept hearing her words over and over in my head. She called my aunt crazy on national television, sitting there laughing at my flesh and blood. A woman I had grown up with. A member of my family and someone I cared deeply about. This wasn't some stranger or even some fictional character on a movie screen. It was my aunt—my deceased aunt who could no longer speak up for herself—and they were disrespecting her memory in front of the entire world.

My aunt passed away before the book was completed, so she never got the chance to speak out about it. She never got the chance to challenge the story told by Rebecca Skloot or the way that she and her family were portrayed. Instead, that so-called journalist took my aunt's death as an opportunity to insert herself into my family's story and make it her own. My Aunt Dale was an intelligent woman and entrepreneur. Yes, she dealt with the pain of losing her mother and her sister, but that didn't mean she was crazy, and it damn sure didn't mean that she deserved to be ridiculed and joked about on a morning news show.

Dale was not crazy. She was a woman who wanted to know the truth about her mother and expose the ill treatment she received during her illness. That wasn't crazy. It was determination.

I was mad as hell after seeing that segment. I went to the phone and called my wife, Hope, at work. I told her about the ridiculousness I had just watched and how they had the nerve to call Dale crazy on TV. My wife wasn't surprised though. She reminded me that it was the same thing we'd been dealing with for the past seven years. That's when I decided this book needed to be written. I needed to reclaim my family's story and my grandmother's legacy. I needed to let the world know what my family truly looked like and what my grandparents did to create a good life for their family. We were not some poor, uneducated, black family in need of pity or saving. We were a proud black family with strong roots and a legacy worth preserving—truthfully.

We've spent years listening to this lady take our story and make it her own. Our family has been split apart by promises of fame, notoriety, and talked into signing away the rights of our own story, only to line the pockets of Rebecca Skloot. My grandmother is studied in college classrooms across the country but belittled in the pages of that book.

It was time to take back our legacy and this book is my way of doing it.

* * *

My grandmother was married to David Lacks, but we all called him Day. Lawrence Lacks is their oldest son and my father. They also had four other children: Lucille "Elsie" Lacks (deceased); David Lacks, Jr., who we all call Sonny; my Aunt Dale; and their youngest Joe Lacks, who later changed his name to Zakiriyya Bari Abdul Rahman. I call him Abdul.

My grandparents worked extremely hard to provide a good life for their children. They instilled a sense of pride and unity in the family that I always appreciated and never thought would go away. I grew up in a home filled with aunts, uncles, and cousins. We celebrated together and supported one another through challenges and tragedies. Even as an adult, my summers were filled with family cook-outs and my winters with holiday gatherings.

My grandfather was a hardworking man, so my father took on a lot of the responsibility as head of the household from a very early age. Everyone respected my father as a leader in my family. Whether they needed to borrow a few dollars or get some good advice, my aunts, uncles, and cousins always came to my father for help. He was smart and hardworking, and we all trusted him to guide the family in the right direction—until Rebecca Skloot came along. She and her book took a close-knit family and split us at the seams.

As family members began to see the appeal of my grandmother's story, they fell to the false promises of notoriety. I feel like they sold their stories, memories, and family for a few thousand dollars and free medical care. We went from family get togethers to arguments... or not speaking at all. Cousins that I was used to seeing on a regular basis didn't even want to take my calls. Children born outside of family marriages and distant cousins who barely ever came around suddenly declared themselves Lacks family representatives. I never imagined that our family would be split up like this. It's sad what people will do for a little bit of money.

From the very beginning of Rebecca Skloot's book, non-fiction went out the window and fiction jumped in. In that first scene, she took it upon herself to describe my grandmother's actions in that bathroom, even though she had no way of verifying what she did or didn't do in there. Nobody knew what happened in that bathroom but Henrietta Lacks. Do you think my grandmother would have wanted her legacy to start with someone making assumptions about her most private moments of pain, fear, and suffering to the whole world? To make a profit, Rebecca Skloot took it upon herself to become Henrietta Lacks' voice in an intimate moment that may not have even occurred, which makes it fiction!

I want to educate the public on the real story.

In interview after interview, Rebecca Skloot referred to my grandparents as poor tobacco farmers. You can look at that famous picture of my grandmother and see that she was not a poor anything. The Lacks family owned their land in Clover, Virginia. She describes our family now as unemployed without any health insurance. I'm sure most families have members without health insurance, and we live in a world where medical and dental costs are too expensive for some people to afford. You don't make that the focus of a whole family though, especially when you're supposed to be writing about the first human cell line to ever grow in culture.

This whole situation has broken my heart, and it's taken a toll on my dad too. I've watched the pain in his eyes over this situation. He misses his family and the connection they used to have. He feels like his mother's soul is not at rest. First, from the continued use of her cells, and now from the lies and inaccuracies spread about our family. My grandmother was a proud woman, and she worked hard to make sure her family was OK, but that's not what the book portrayed.

Rebecca Skloot's book and the HBO film painted us as poor and ignorant, which couldn't be further from the truth. We were a middle-class family. My dad was an engineer for the Conrail Railroad where he retired from. He always carried himself with class and respect, taking charge and caring for his whole family. But that's not what readers of the book will learn about his life.

She conveniently left out family members who challenged her story, wiping us out as if we didn't even exist. Instead, she focused on the people who were willing to sell out the entire family at the first sight of a few coins. She took my father, the oldest child and the only one who actually remembered my grandmother, and almost completely removed him from the story. The first time he read the manuscript for the book, he told Rebecca Skloot that some of things weren't true. But her response to him was... it's not your book! She also went out of her way to defame my mother and make her look like some rude and angry tyrant, which she isn't. She is a proud and intelligent black woman who saw right through Rebecca Skloot's bullshit. I have people calling my phone, wanting to donate money to the family. My wife and I refused to take money from people who themselves were suffering and needed the money more than we did. We have always been a family to take care of our own and we always will be. But this is not the image that people have of Henrietta's family legacy. Instead they have been fed a very disappointing and disturbing image, written by a woman who claims to speak for us.

I know some people wonder why I take such issue with the story. So many people have told me that the portrayal of my family doesn't matter, as long as the Henrietta Lacks story was told. But it really does matter to us. Because this is history... the Henrietta Lacks family history and, yes, it matters a lot!

We think the public has a right to know what has happened to the Lacks family since Skloot's book came out, and it's not what people think. I am writing this book to tell the truth. I want my grandmother's story told from the perspective of the people who knew her best—not from the view of some woman who inserts herself into the story, or from distant relatives seeking to profit off our family name.

My grandmother's story is one that deserves to be told truthfully and accurately—and not at the expense of our family's name. That is the type of pride that my grandmother passed down to my father and the type of pride that my father and mother passed down to me. So, I will tell this story. I'm not worried about whose feelings get hurt or who doesn't like what I have to say. This is about truth and reclaiming the Lacks family legacy.

Henrietta Lacks

Lucile Elsie Lacks (Courtesy of Joyce Foster)

David Lacks

David and Henrietta Lacks

2

FROM CLOVER TO BALTIMORE

My grandmother's life began in Roanoke, Virginia, in 1920. After the death of her mother in 1924, she was moved to Clover, Virginia, where she lived until moving to Baltimore, Maryland, in 1941. She spent most of her childhood with her grandfather, Tommy Lacks, in an area of Clover called Lackstown. They lived in a big log cabin that I would see on my visits to Clover. It's all boarded up though, so I never got to go inside. The family said it used to be part of the plantation, which was once owned by Henrietta's white great-grandfather.

Henrietta's parents were named John and Eliza Pleasant. I don't know too much about either of them, except that Eliza died at the age of 38. John worked for the railroads in Roanoke until his wife passed away. That's when he moved his children back to Lackstown where his father, Tommy, raised them.

My grandmother started working in the tobacco fields at a young age, which was normal back in those days. Henrietta had her first child, my father, at fourteen years old. Four years later, her daughter Elsie was born. My father says she was a normal little girl, until some kind of accident happened, which left her with developmental disabilities. I've never gotten a full explanation of her condition because my dad doesn't talk about it too much. The family always just said that she was "different."

My grandparents grew up in the same house, with a bunch of other cousins. Rebecca Skloot tried to portray their relationship as evil and incestuous, but you have to look at it in the context of that time. I mean, I know you can't really clean that up. But in that era, and under those circumstances, it was not an <u>uncommon thing</u> for second cousins to <u>marry and have families.</u> We're talking about the 1920s. Black people could not just come and go as they pleased. They weren't able to move around much, so they really only knew the people who they grew up with, which were usually close and distant cousins. In fact, in the late 1800s and early 1900s, it was common for rural people of all races to marry cousins. In my opinion, Rebecca Skloot only mentioned this part of our family history to fit her goal of trying to make my grandparents look ignorant.

My father practically grew up with my grandmother, and he's the only child with any memory of her life before the move to Maryland. His eyes still light up when he talks about the good times with his mama. I can tell that he not only loved her, but he respected her as a person.

Henrietta He shared stories of a young, fun-loving country girl, who could get down in the dirt with the best of them. He said they would go horseback riding, swimming, and have cookouts in the yard. My grandmother was also pretty good at fishing—and she did it often, catching dinner and bringing it home to fry up for the family. She would even help my father haul pails of water from the creek so they could do the laundry. My dad remembers a vibrant and happy woman who loved to be physically active. He said she was always athletic and in good shape… until her illness.

My dad's fondest memories were of them sitting in the front yard by the fire pit, looking up at the stars. She amazed him with her knowledge of the constellations, pointing out the Big and Little Dippers, Orion's Belt, and others. He said it was fun sitting in the yard with his mother at night. It was their special time and he smiles a lot when he speaks about it.

Sometimes, other family members would come by and gather in that Clover front yard. They would share memories and tell stories and laugh. My dad said they would sometimes talk about the white side of the Lacks family, who owned a lot of the land that they all settled on. He doesn't remember a lot of what was said about them, but he doesn't recall ever hearing anything bad. Henrietta's white grandfather left them a nice piece of land to farm and raise their family, and they saw that as generous.

My dad says he can still hear his mom's big infectious laugh echoing through his memories. He said it was distinct and no one had a laugh like hers. He recalled waking up in the darkness of the old house and sometimes feeling afraid, until he heard his mother's laughter. She loved to laugh and when something was really funny to her, and it would bring tears to her eyes. He said that she was always confident and sure of herself. If her husband, Day, had to be away from home, my grandmother would take charge of the house without missing a beat, making sure that my father and his sister were looked after. When she would go out and work in the tobacco fields, my father would watch Elsie.

I've been told that my grandfather loved my grandmother very much and even he was in awe of her strength and character. He married her in April 1941, and they moved to Maryland about a year later. Day's cousin helped him get a job at Bethlehem Steel and they eventually moved into their own house in Turner Station, an area that they call Dundalk now.

Back then, Turner Station was one of the largest African American communities in Baltimore County. A lot of black men found jobs with Bethlehem Steel, making decent money, but they weren't allowed to purchase land in Sparrow Point, where the factory was located. So, they found a small area in Turner Station and created a community for themselves. It wasn't some dilapidated area of poor, uneducated blacks. It was a thriving community of businesses and families with schools, churches, grocery stores, and beauty shops. Doctors opened offices in this area. Restaurants, dentists, gas stations, liquor stores, and clothing stores sprung up and prospered around the Turner Station. It was a community of black middle class and Day worked hard to provide a place for his family there.

That's why it makes me so mad to see how Rebecca Skloot portrayed by grandmother and grandfather in her book. White people have a different history from us, and their perspective of a good family life is different. She judged my family based on her history and experiences as a white woman in America, not based on the history and experiences of a black family only a couple of generations out of slavery. My grandparents may not have been wealthy, but Day did everything he could to provide for his family. I've heard stories of him working fifteen acres of tobacco by himself in Clover. I resent Rebecca Skloot, and everyone involved in that movie, for minimizing that.

My dad says that the move to the city changed my grandmother. In Clover, she had been relaxed and less strict with my father, but after moving to Baltimore, she became much more protective. She took care of the house while my grandfather worked at the shipyard, earning pretty good money. My grandfather was always a hard worker, and he was away from home a lot. During that time, my dad took on a lot of responsibilities around the house.

When it was time to go out on the town, Henrietta went all out—all dressed up in her best clothes, looking like a movie star out of a magazine. She was very classy and loved going out to the local nightclub to see entertainers like Billie Holiday and Cab Calloway. Back then, Pennsylvania Avenue was the place to go for entertainment and fun. My dad said Henrietta loved to dance and her drink of choice was vodka and orange juice.

She did miss her family and Clover though. She never really got used to the compact living that comes along with a row house. Not that she wasn't a people person, she was just used to the open spaces of Clover. In Clover, she was surrounded by family all the time. After moving to Baltimore, she had to wait for family to visit, which is why she loved Christmas time so much, because that's when more family would come to visit. My grandparents would also open their home to folks from Clover who were moving to Baltimore themselves, allowing them to stay there while saving enough money to get their own homes. My dad remembers watching his mom play cards and horseshoes with friends and family during their visits. Henrietta and Day were gracious and generous people who loved their family.

My grandparents had three more children after moving to Maryland. Sonny was born in 1947, Dale was born in 1949, and Abdul was born in 1950. It was right after Abdul's birth that Henrietta was diagnosed with cervical cancer.

My dad doesn't like to talk about my grandmother's illness. It makes him too sad to think about. He told Rebecca Skloot that he didn't remember much, but that wasn't true. He really didn't like the idea of her writing a book about his family. He doesn't like talking about it, but he definitely remembers a lot. He told me that, as my grandmother became weaker, it got harder for her to care for Elsie, and my grandparents had to place her in a mental hospital where she stayed until her death in 1955. That was an awful situation there. My dad talks about how distraught and heartbroken his mother was behind that decision. She did not want to give up her daughter, but her illness made it almost impossible to care for her. My dad said that he could see how badly it broke her heart to place Elsie in that place.

My grandmother always instilled the importance of taking care of family to my dad. With Day working all the time, my dad took care of the children a lot after his mother became ill. That never changed either. Even decades later, my dad was pretty much the head of the household, helping everyone and taking care of his siblings. He was like a second father to all of them.

It was in 1951 when my grandmother was first diagnosed by Dr. Howard Jones at Johns Hopkins Hospital. To understand how big of a deal this was, you have to understand the climate of that time. Black people were scared of Johns Hopkins. There were stories and rumors of black people being abducted from around Hopkins at night and used for medical experiments. African Americans wouldn't go to Johns Hopkins Hospital for anything in those days. Instead they would go to City Hospital because they didn't trust the Johns Hopkins doctors. It's a different situation today. They have reached out to the family to try and make amends; I think most of us do go there now. Both of my parents have received treatment at Johns Hopkins, and they were treated really well as descendants of Henrietta Lacks. But that doesn't erase the hospital's legacy of racism within the African American community. My sister LaDonna still won't go to Johns Hopkins today.

For my grandmother to go there for treatment, she was really in some serious pain. According to reports I've seen, Dr. Jones said that my grandmother's general examination came out fine. But when he did the vaginal exam, he could actually see the lesion on her cervix. He said it wasn't like anything he'd seen before, or ever again saw after. Dr. Jones took a biopsy of a mass on her cervix and diagnosed her with a malignant epidermoid carcinoma of the cervix. That ended up being the wrong diagnosis though, and, in 1970, some doctors discovered that what she actually had was something called an adenocarcinoma.

The doctors treated my grandmother with radium tube inserts. That means she endured a radiation bar being inserted into her vagina. Dr. Jones called her cells "unstoppable" because they did not respond well to the treatment. After the treatments, she was discharged and sent home. According to my dad, the house started to feel sad when she came home. Within a short period of time, my grand-mother went from this vibrant, energetic, beautiful woman to someone almost unrecognizable. Her physical appear-ance changed tremendously, which deeply disturbed my dad. He wasn't used to seeing his mother unkempt and in such a weakened state.

He said the family started grieving way before her death, with cousins and family friends coming by to see her one last time. They would often discuss their concerns about Henrietta and Johns Hopkins. They were worried about the doctors' intentions. Black folks did not get that kind of attention back then. They would bring up a whole bunch of conspiracy theories about what they were doing to Henrietta. The family had known other people who had cancer, but this seemed different. She was receiving a lot of attention from the doctors at Johns Hopkins, which was highly unusual for a black woman at that time. They all felt like there were too many doctors attending to her. They had very little trust in the medical profession and even less in Johns Hopkins, so to have her in the hospital so much and for so long felt wrong and raised their suspicions. We didn't have any rights back then and the family could barely get any information about Henrietta. Shoot, we barely have any rights today. When we tried to get information about my grandmother, we were turned away and even threat-ened with legal action. Yet, it seems like some people are more than able to walk into Johns Hopkins and get infor-mation whenever they wanted it. It's ridiculous.

My dad said that the family didn't even feel comfortable waiting inside the hospital while his mother received treatments. They were treated like second-hand citizens that didn't have any right to be there. My dad would take his siblings to sit in the car until their father came out of the hospital. He would come out with tears in his eyes and would have to get himself together before he could drive off.

According to my dad, all the joy eventually left their home. The smell of illness replaced the aromas of good cooking that used to fill up the entire house. Some family friends say that they could hear Henrietta's painful cries all throughout the neighborhood. It was an extremely sad and stressful situation for everyone, but especially my father. Towards the end, my dad remembers having to feed his mother because she was too weak to feed herself. He says that she had rashes and sores all over her body, and her sweet perfume scent was replaced with bodily odors of sickness. She constantly talked about her children and worried about them being taken care of, but he felt like she had made her peace with God.

On August 8, 1951, my grandmother went to Johns Hopkins for a routine treatment session. She was in severe pain. They gave her blood transfusions and kept her in the hospital until her death on October 4, 1951. She was 31 years old and my father was 16 years old. On her death- bed, my father remembers that she wanted him and Day to promise that Johns Hopkins wouldn't get her body.

Even in her last hours, she remembered all the rumors about body snatching. She also talked about all the attention she was getting from the doctors and how strange it all seemed. She wanted her body taken back to Clover to be buried, and it was, but my father feels that his mother still isn't at rest.

What no one knew at the time was that two cell samples were taken from my grandmother's body during those hospital treatments. One sample was of healthy tissue and the other was cancerous tissue. The cancerous cells became known as the HeLa cell line. They wanted to hide that my grandmother was the source of the cells, so they used the first two letters of her first and last names. That cell line has since become one of the most commonly used cell lines in contemporary medical research.

On the day my grandmother died, George Otto Gey—a biologist at Johns Hopkins—went on national television show, called *Cancer Can Be Conquered*, with a vial of my grandmother's cells. He had been trying to grow human cells inside test tubes for twenty years because he thought he could identify the cause of cancer in the tubes. Calling my grandmother's cells HeLa, he said, "It is possible that, from a fundamental study such as this, we will be able to learn a way by which cancer can be completely wiped out." So, while my grandmother's body lay in the morgue, George Gey, was proclaiming his plans to use her cells— and none of my family members knew anything about it. Even more insulting, while he was on TV, his assistant was at the morgue collecting more cells from my grandmother's body. She said that she could see tumors all over my grandmother's abdomen.

* * *

My grandmother was buried in Clover, as she wished. Henrietta was buried near her mother's grave. My dad went to her funeral, but he couldn't bring himself to go to the burial ground. He said he didn't want to see that. My father went through a lot during Henrietta's last months. She was almost unrecognizable at her death. She went from a vibrant woman to a skeleton of herself and my dad, being sixteen years old, he took that hard. I can understand how he felt because I went through something similar with the death of my mother's father. After his cancer diagnosis, I would go visit him with my mother. He was always a big guy, but I remember that he looked like a skeleton with skin. Seeing that does something to you as a child.

So, now as my father is getting older, I'm trying to get bits and pieces of Henrietta's story from him when he feels like talking. His memories seem to come in spurts. While he doesn't like talking about the hard times, he always gets happy when talking about his mother before her illness. It's been wonderful getting to know my grandmother through my dad's memories and I hope the whole world will have a different perspective about her and our family once they read his stories and learn what really happened.

David (Sonny) Lacks – taking selfies before it was cool!

Bobbette Lacks

Lawrence Lacks

3

A HAPPY CHILDHOOD

was about thirteen years old when I took my first trip to Lackstown. My grandfather used to take me and my sister down there in the summers. School would let out, then we would head down there for a couple of months. I remember that, as a child, it felt like such a long ride. I was a city boy and it was strange to see nothing but trees on that four-hour journey. I just wanted to get there, but it seemed like we would never stop seeing trees. Once we got to Clover, we turned off the highway onto this dirt road. I'll never forget the sound of the dirt kicking up from the wheels of our car.

As we continued down the dirt road, houses sporadically came into view and I remember my grandfather telling us that they all belonged to family members. Day would say your uncle lives there, pointing at one house, and your cousin lives over there, pointing to another house. Family was all around us. No matter who you are, when your car comes down that dirt road, you are getting a wave— and it seemed like everyone knew Day. I will always remember that about Clover—people were so friendly. We didn't even stay with Day when we were down there. I stayed with one relative and my sister stayed with another relative, but we knew we would be well taken care of.

We'd always go to Honey's house first. Honey was like the Rockefeller of the Lacks family, having bought up a bunch of the land down there. When we stopped at her house, she came out to greet Day with her bellowing voice. She wasn't necessarily a nice woman to children, but I could tell she liked and respected Day. Honey was something else, a short, rounded woman with some age on her. She struck me as an in-charge type of person. I can still hear her yelling out, "Hey Day! Pull on up. Pull your car right here. We in the house!" Honey commanded attention and respect. On my first trip to her house, I didn't know anybody, but I remember that there were a lot of kids. They knew we were from Baltimore and they all excitedly came to greet us. I remember feeling so welcomed.

Honey had two daughters who were about my age. It was like having instant friends. We would go and do some of the simplest things, but it was so much fun, like walking to the creek or messing with the livestock—cows and bulls and stuff. They knew about the animals, but I was a city slicker. I wasn't messing with any of those animals. I wouldn't even go up to a chicken until I got used to it. They sure teased me about it too, but I teased them back for talking so slow and country. I remember they would try to get me to ride the horses with them, but I wouldn't. That horse was too big, and I was scared to climb up there. In fact, even with all those summers in Clover, I was a grown man before I ever got on a horse.

I'll never forget my first morning waking up in Clover. We had eggs, bacon, squash, and biscuits for breakfast. Lord, have mercy. That breakfast was so good. I have loved squash for breakfast ever since then. All these decades later, and I have never forgotten the taste of that break-fast. That's how good it was.

Day took us to see the "home house." That's what they called the house that he and Henrietta lived in. It looked like a wooden shed, but it was a nice-sized building. It was about 30 feet by 40 feet, something like that. Over the years, it had fallen into disarray. My grandfather would tell me how he used to farm the land and how happy he and Henrietta had been there. Just like my dad, he often told us about how much our grandmother loved riding horses.

The night sky in Clover is ingrained in my head. It was so dark that you couldn't see your hand in front of your face, but the sky was filled with stars. It was surreal and beautiful. As a Baltimore boy, I was used to night skies filled with streetlights and the lights peering through brownstone windows. But in Clover, there were no streetlights. I was amazed by that. The only light came from the moon and the stars in the sky. We would lay on the ground with a corn pipe and gaze out into the sky. Being in the city, you don't have space like that, where you can lie on the ground at night and feel comfortable and safe. In Clover, it seemed like we had the whole sky to ourselves as a family. There were no strangers around, just family.

As I recall, my mother went down to Clover twice. She and Honey didn't get along too well. I think it was because they were both very strong women. My mom also wasn't one for going down to the creek to get water. She hated all those mosquitos down there. Trying to impress my mom, the men folk would go get fresh water for her sometimes. They didn't care if she was married to my dad or not; they loved to flirt with her. There was one guy, his name was Gus. I'm not sure how he was related, but he and my mom got along well. He would go down to the creek to get water for her, and my mom would give him a couple of dollars to say thanks.

The kids liked to pick on Gus. At night, when he was sleeping, we would take rocks and throw them on top of his tin roof. It would scare him to death, and he would come running out hollering at us while we ran away laughing. We would only do that with Gus though. Anybody else would have come out with their shotguns blazing, so we knew who to do that to and who to leave alone.

During those summers in Lackstown, I found out that everybody knew about my grandmother, and they all had such good things to say about her. She was always there for family members in need, sharing whatever she had with them. She and my grandfather didn't have a lot of money, but they shared whatever they had. I also learned that she always wanted her children to get an education. That's another thing that makes me so mad about Rebecca Skloot's book. It stated that my grandmother couldn't read or write and had to sign her name with an "X." I feel like that is a racist, stereotypical lie. We had to pull up the proof that Henrietta could not only write, but that she even wrote in cursive. The writer was trying to portray my family in a certain way, but they had to change their description from illiterate to limited reading abilities, once they knew that I had shown some news reports the documents of my grandmother signing her own name. While my grandmother did not finish school, she wasn't illiterate. She would even help my father with his schoolwork when he was growing up.

I also heard about Henrietta's partying days on those visits to Clover. She and her cousins would throw parties at this local shack, where they would play music and cook delicious food. Cousins and friends would come from all over to attend their parties. Who would have thought that, decades later, I would party in that same shack?

I was in my late teens when my cousin and I packed up my dad's van with some Maryland chicken, cases of beer, and my entire stereo system. We decided that we would throw a party in Clover and make some money down there at the same time. We cleaned out the shack and threw a big event. People were in there dancing and having a good time. We partied that whole weekend. There were a few hiccups that first night though. We were frying the chicken as people ordered it, but we didn't expect them to be ordering like crazy. We got way behind and spent the whole night cooking chicken. By Saturday, we had it together though. We made the chicken ahead of time that day. Cars were pulling up from everywhere and we all had such a good time. I remember stopping in the middle of the party and thinking about the fact that this was where my grandparents used to party too. I imagined what kind of music they played back then. They didn't have electricity, so they must have used candles and lanterns to light the shack. I imagined them dancing together in the same space where I was standing.

Sometimes, Day would take me to Halifax, Virginia, to stay with my boy cousins, Tommy and them. It almost felt like the city when I visited them. They had one of those manufactured homes and it was huge. It looked like a modern house, with a pond out back and a wooden fence pen holding in their bull. Tommy drove a Nova and he would take us riding to visit more of our people. There wasn't any mall or movie theater or anything like that. It was just gathering with folks. As we got older, we would ride and go to the beaches down there. I remember I almost drowned on one of those trips. It makes me laugh just thinking about it now.

My Aunt Dale and I were playing in the water and the waves had us bouncing around. I didn't realize we had bounced over to an area where the seafloor sloped down.

We both took a step and, all of a sudden, the water was above our heads. She couldn't swim as well as I could, so she was on top of my head trying to keep her head above water, but she almost drowned me in the process. I was trying to hold her up and walk back to shallower water at the same time, but she was holding onto my head so tight that I could barely keep myself afloat. Finally, someone came and grabbed her off me, but instead of me popping up, I went farther under. I probably took in about a gallon of water before I finally came up for air. And when I finally got myself together, not a single soul was even looking to see if I was OK. While they were all worried about Dale, I was out there drowning. It's funny now, but I was scared to death at the time.

I was a fish though. Both of my parents made sure I could swim. Every other weekend, they would put my siblings and me in the car and take us to Gunpowder Beach on the Chesapeake Bay. A bunch of family and friends would all meet there for a day of swimming, playing, and fun. Aside from Clover, those days at Gunpowder Beach are some of my fondest childhood memories.

We lived in East Baltimore during that time, and the house was filled with family. Day, my parents, Sonny, Dale, and Abdul all lived in that house. My aunts and uncles were right there with me as a child. Family was all around in that house. I remember my Uncle Abdul liked to mess with us younger kids, taking his chin and pushing it into our heads.

Then, Sonny would take him outside and whip his tail for messing with us.

My mom didn't like that neighborhood because it was in a pretty rough part of town. I was maybe seven or eight, sitting in the yard eating a sweet slice of watermelon, when a beer bottle came flying through the air and hit the watermelon, just inches from my head. My mother was so mad that she was ready to hurt somebody. That day, she told my father that we had to move away from the neighborhood. My dad knew she was serious, so he did what he had to do and moved us to Kitmore Road. That was a nice, beautiful neighborhood.

It was a good upbringing and we never wanted for anything. My mother was a strong disciplinarian, and she was serious about her kids doing right. She didn't spare the belt. We all got spankings and I definitely got my fair share of tail whippings. I remember my cousins would come over and spend the night all the time. And when one of us got in trouble, all of us got spanked equally. I would always try to go last, hoping she would be too tired by the time she got to me.

Going down to Virginia was a fun vacation from Baltimore. But that's not how Rebecca Skloot's book portrayed it. She made Lackstown look like a bunch of poor black folks, but that's not what I saw or felt during those summers. Nobody was scratching and going hungry. They were just living their lives, going about their daily chores and relaxing on their porches in the evening. They didn't have a care in the world as they sipped on their corn liquor and ate their fresh oranges. I never even experienced racism when I was down there. To tell the truth, I wasn't even raised with racism. I didn't know anything about it. I was a teenager before I learned anything about the hatred between white and black. I had been taking a drivers ed class that evening. It was a cold night and I was waiting for the bus to go home. I was about to freeze, so I went into this inn to try and warm up. When the owner saw me, he fussed at me and threw me out into the cold. That was my first experience with racism.

I stopped going down to Lackstown when I thought I was too grown to go. I decided it was more important to spend the summers with my friends than to take those trips to Virginia. I've visited a few times as an adult, and I still feel like I'm surrounded by family whenever I'm there. For me, Clover is so much more than some little country town in Virginia. It's my grandmother's heart, her essence, and part of her legacy. Clover will always have a special place in my heart.

My family in Atlantic City

Ron Lacks – Boy Scouts

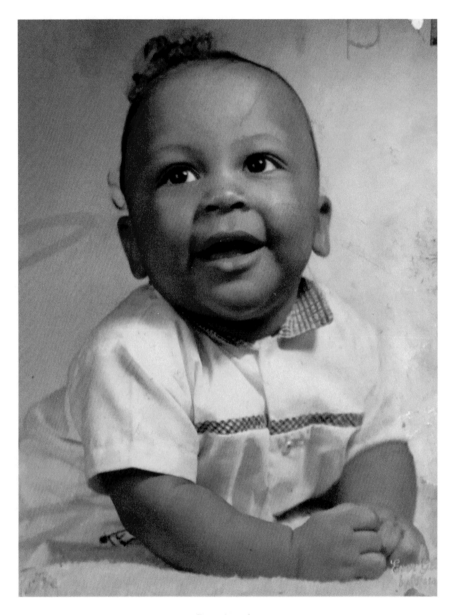

Ron Lacks

Ron and LaDonna Lacks

4

MY GRANDMOTHER'S IMMORTALITY

We first learned about my grandmother's cells when I was about sixteen years old, almost a quarter of a century after her death. My mom had brunch with a friend, her friend's sister, and the sister's husband who was a scientist from Washington, D.C. After being introduced to my mom, the scientist commented that her name sounded familiar. He told her that he'd been working with some cells in his lab called HeLa, which came from a woman named Henrietta Lacks. He asked her if she was related. My mom told him that Henrietta Lacks was her husband's mother, and that she had been deceased for almost 24 years. My mom didn't know what he meant by working with her cells and the news had her a bit shook. When she asked him to explain, he told her that the cells, which had been alive since Henrietta's death, were being used by scientists worldwide. He told her that they were, in fact, so widely used that most of the world's molecular scientists had been working with them at one time or another.

My mom couldn't wait to tell my dad what she'd been told. She didn't even finish her food. Instead, she excused herself and got home as fast as she could. She told my dad that his mom's cells were still alive and explained what the scientist had told her, but neither of them really understood what was happening. My dad called the family together to tell them about the cells. Now, everybody was confused. They wanted to know what it meant for the cells to still be alive and why no one ever told them about it. The family was still in Baltimore and some of us had been to Johns Hopkins for treatment during that time. They could have easily gotten in touch with us if they wanted to. That's when stories and theories about my grandmother's cells started going around the whole family.

My mom called Johns Hopkins a bunch of times to try and find out what was going on with the cells. She even got some attorneys to try and see what was happening, but they couldn't get anything out of the hospital either. We never got any information at all. Even worse, they never gave us any credible reason for *not* telling us anything. They would just explain that in 1951, they were under no obligation to tell black people anything... not even Henrietta's husband. We were probably asking the same questions that Rebecca Skloot would eventually ask. Yet, we couldn't get any answers. But when she asked, they told her everything she wanted to know. That just doesn't sit right with me. You keep information from the immediate family—Henrietta's direct descendants—but you freely hand it over to a lady with no connection at all to the family. We were told that all of the records about Henrietta were locked in a vault at Johns Hopkins. So, what made them so eager to share this highly protected information with some writer.

I don't exactly know how *Rolling Stone* and *Jet* magazines came about doing their stories. I just came home from school one day and a reporter from *Rolling Stone* was in the house doing an interview with Day, my mother, my dad, and my sister. When they interviewed me, I didn't really understand what it was all about, but I knew it was something special about my grandmother. I had no clue about the importance of it until the article came out and I started reading about the cells.

That's why it bothers me when I see family members speaking at different universities, making these false statements that they didn't know anything about Henrietta or the HeLa cells until the book came out. That just isn't true. They did know. How could they possibly not know the history of the family when it was in so many different magazines and local papers for so many years? The fact that they could just put that false information out there like that is unbelievable to me.

I remember reading about a woman named Helen Lane, and that she was the topic of some science paper that "sent tremors through the whole structure of international medical research." I didn't know what any of that meant, but I kept reading, hoping it would start to make sense. The *Rolling Stone* writer talked about George Gey and his wife, who were trying to grow human cells in a glass dish. All gibberish to me. Then, he mentioned a young black woman from Baltimore who walked into Johns Hopkins and how a gynecologist took some of the lesions from her body to George Gey. I'm thinking, "OK, is he talking about my grandmother now?" But then he started talking about this Helen Lane woman again. He wrote about how the HeLa cells were contaminating entire laboratories. In fact, it wasn't until three-fourths of the way through the story that I finally read my grandmother's name.

Quoting George Gey's wife, the author wrote, "Henrietta Lacks. That was her real name. I don't think anybody is quite sure how everybody got to calling her Helen Lane." Now, I'm shocked. All this time, the Helen Lane that he was describing was actually my grandmother. Next, he started talking about my dad and grandfather. He talked about sitting across the table from Day at my dad's house, and how Day was confused about when they took the cells from her body. Nobody asked him about taking cells from her body until after her death, even though they already had them before she died. I mean, how could George Gey already have the cells in his possession as my grandmother lay in a cold morgue?

Next, the article went on to talk about my father. It talked about how the family had been contacted by someone asking to come and take blood samples from the children and grandchildren. I remember when that happened. Some Johns Hopkins nurses came to the house and took blood from all the siblings. They wanted samples from me and my siblings too, but my mother said no. We never did learn exactly what they did with those samples. The nurses told the family that they were worried about them having the same illness as Henrietta, but men can't get that, so it was just some off-the-wall excuse.

My mom used to call the hospital a lot, asking about the status of Henrietta's cells and the blood samples that were taken, but she never got any responses. When we couldn't get any answers, we started to get fearful about what they wanted to do with the cells. According to the *Rolling Stone* article, HeLa cells could contaminate every-thing. What if they tried to weaponize them and were using Henrietta's cells to do harm? We just wanted answers, but they never really came.

In fact, I'm still not 100% clear about what they did with the blood samples they collected from my dad and his siblings. I've read a few articles that mention genetic markers that they found in our DNA, but we still don't have any straight answers. I also read that they used the blood samples to study genetic mapping. From what I under-stand, that is where they try to link the transmission of dis-eases from parent to child with genes and chromosomes.

I suspect that they were hoping to find some clues about why my grandmother's cells are so resilient.

As a sixteen-year-old teenager, the *Rolling Stone* article was a big deal in the neighborhood. My family became a little famous. People were asking me about my grandmother and talking about the article. It was a real boost to my popularity, and I latched onto it and played it the hilt. The kids at school were acting like I was some kind of celebrity or something.

Then, right when things started calming down, the *Jet* magazine article came out. Now, I have to admit that I didn't know much about *Rolling Stone*, but I knew about *Jet*. All black people knew about *Jet*, and being in it was big time. It was for black readers and all the neighbors saw the article. Being in *Jet* meant we'd hit the big time. Going through the halls at school, people would be staring at me and asking, "What's up with that?" I was the big man on campus, and I loved it.

While I was the big man on campus, I wasn't the big man at home. As I started smelling myself, I began doing some of the stupid things that teenagers do. I remember one time, my friend Charles and I cut school to hang out. We went to my Aunt Dale's house, thinking that she wouldn't tell on us. It was the end of the school year and a lot of kids were leaving school early. This was actually our second day skipping. We had gotten away with it the day before, so we figured we'd do it again. For some reason, we decided to go hang out at Dale's house. It was the time of day when she should have been at home, but she didn't come to the door, even when we kept knocking. We figured that she had gone somewhere and would be coming right back, so we decided to just wait. They had one of those air conditioner units out front and we sat on it to wait for her. We were just sitting there talking and laughing, just happy to not be in school.

After about a half an hour, I looked up and here comes my mother's car rolling up in the parking lot. I was busted! My mom started fussing at me, yelling, "What are you doing out of school?! You are supposed to be in school! Get in this car!" So, we walked to the car like we were headed to the electric chair. Then, I looked back at Dale's apartment and saw her curtain open a little bit. She had been in there the whole time and ratted me out. I was so mad at her back then, but I laugh about it now. That was just the kind of stuff that went on between Dale and me. She was like the big sister who was constantly looking out for me, even when I didn't want her to.

Dale stayed with us several times throughout my life. She helped raise me. She even saved my life a couple of times. Once, when I was small, I was in the backyard where we had this pole with a rope hanging from it. I wrapped the rope around my neck and was swinging from it. Dale came running outside and snatched that rope from around my neck. I can still hear her yelling, "You're gonna kill yourself boy!" I probably would have accidentally strangled myself to death in that backyard if it hadn't been for Dale looking out for me.

My mom, Barbara "Bobette" Lacks, is such an intelligent woman. She is strong and classy. She always stood up for her family and wouldn't let anyone disrespect any of us. She treated Dale as her own, helping and supporting her through all kinds of things. That's why Rebecca Skloot's book bothered my mother so much. Remember, my mom was the first one to really hear about Henrietta's cells and I think God did that on purpose. He knew that my mom had the drive and intelligence to pursue the situation and seek out answers. But the book tried to portray my mother as some angry woman with a bad attitude. I mean, the writer took the mad black woman stereotype to the max when writing about my mom. Even the way they portrayed her in the movie made her look like a hateful, bitter woman. But that's not my mother at all. Yes, she was skeptical of Rebecca Skloot; I mean, here comes this woman coming around asking questions. My mom questioned her motives, and it turns out that she was absolutely right to do so.

My mother was an entrepreneur and a very smart businesswoman. She and my father met each other when they were young. One story my mom told me always makes me laugh. My dad drove a gold Impala back then. When my mom brought him to meet her grandmother, her grandmother said, "I don't know about him. His eyes are the same color as his car." Obviously, my mom decided that my dad was the one for her. They moved in together in 1959. My dad was 24 and my mom was just 20. My mom quickly became a part of the Lacks family. She and Day were super close. I don't think any father-in-law and daughter-inlaw ever got along better than the two of them. Even though she was relatively young herself, she took on the role of woman of the house. At first it was just my mom, dad, and Day. Then, I eventually came along. But my mom also took on the role of taking care of my dad's siblings, and she did it without any hesitation.

That's one thing Rebecca Skloot actually got right in the book. After Henrietta's death, Day sent the youngest kids to live with some cousins, Ethel and Garland. I've heard stories about the abuse they unleashed on those kids. Some of my elder family members said that Ethel had a thing for Day, and she was jealous of his relationship with my grandmother. They said Ethel hated Henrietta and she took that hatred out on her children. She refused to give them food and beat them for her own enjoyment, hitting them for no reason at all. From what I've been told, she especially hated Abdul and he got the worst of her torture. She used to make him stand up against the wall, tying him up with rope while she whipped him across his back like a slave.

With all that he endured, it's no wonder Abdul had so many problems as an adult. He was born in the midst of his mother's cancer and had to fight tuberculosis for the first year of his life. Then, to experience such hatred and abuse as an innocent child... it's heartbreaking. I remember that Abdul used to drink a lot and he was always angry, sometimes for no reason at all. He joined the military, but he would constantly get into fights with the other soldiers. They eventually declared him psychologically unfit to serve and discharged him. A while later, he was convicted of murdering a man and served fifteen years. That's when he found Islam and changed his name. Abdul's involvement with Rebecca Skloot's book was limited. I think he did talk to her about some things because I heard stories about him and Dale going to Johns Hopkins, but Abdul mostly kept to himself. He didn't have the patience for arguments and drama.

My mother found out about the abuse being done to my dad's siblings after Garland tried to rape Dale. Without missing a beat, she went over to that house and demanded that the kids be given to her—and she raised them from that day forward. That's why they all have a level of respect for my mom and her opinion. She had raised them since they were kids. We all grew up in the house together.

I'm my mother's oldest child. She's the kind of mother who loves unconditionally, but she didn't play. I remember one time I was supposed to rake the leaves up, or something else, and I was slow getting out of bed to get it done. When I finally got up, I found that my mom had packed my bags, placed them by the front door and called the police on me. She told them, "I want him out my damn house!" They escorted me away from the house too. So, here I am on the corner, sitting on my suitcase saying to myself, "Why didn't I just get them damn leaves up?" I think my maternal grandmother called somebody to come get me, so I wasn't out there too long, but I never forgot that. My mom just wanted to show me who was boss. I always respected and loved my mom. Some people might think that was abusive, but it wasn't. My mom came from a time when sparing the rod meant spoiling the child, and she wasn't about raising any spoiled children. I'm glad I got what I got from my mom.

Ironically enough, she took it light on her grandchildren. That shocked me because I knew how my mom was when we were growing up. I couldn't believe she let them get away with some of the stuff they did, like walking around her house and refusing to speak to her. It upsets me even now to know that she was walking around in her own house and they were disrespecting her like that. I just wish I had realized what was going on earlier so I could have done something about it, but I didn't know just how much pressure she was under. I thought she was fine, but she was actually over there dealing with some serious issues.

About a month before her stroke, my mom called and asked me to take her to the store. She couldn't drive around like she used to. It was the first time she'd asked that of me. I picked her up and took her to the store. We had such a lovely time. We talked and laughed.

She wasn't just my mom. She was like a friend. That was totally different for me, and I enjoyed that time so much. When I got home, I bragged about it to my wife.

Then, I called and excitedly told my father. I was like, "Dad, guess what. I just took my mom to the store and we had such a good time." I was looking forward to doing it again but before that could happen, she had her stroke.

My mom passed out on the floor of her kitchen. After her stroke, she was in a nursing home for a while. She and my dad were already separated, but I couldn't let her stay there. I didn't want to make any waves, but when I saw what they were doing to my mom, I could not take it. Every time I'd go up there to visit, she was drugged up and completely out of it. She was on about ten different pills. They would have them all lined up and I would always ask why she was taking so many pills. That's when I brought her from the nursing home into my home.

My brother and sister barely come to see her, so it can be really challenging sometimes, but she is my priority and I cherish the time that I do have with her. I try to take good care of her. I found out that those medications were for all sorts of preventable conditions, but since my mom has been with me, she has been weaned off of all that. I was able to regulate her vitals and get her off of all those medications. Now, aside from her vitamins, she does not take one pill. Even the doctors were surprised by how well she was doing. When they see she's not on any medication, they get to pulling out that blood pressure machine, but every time, they find out that her blood pressure is spot on. For the last seven years, my mother has not had any blood pressure problems. That's my mom, and as long as I can physically take care of her, I will.

I didn't know anything about it until after my mom's stroke, but my wife and my mother had a few conversations about me. My mother told my wife that she was proud of me. I had just bought my first house and I was really getting myself together. It made me so happy to hear that. I wanted my mother to be proud of her oldest son. I miss the vibrant woman my mother was before the stroke and I know she wouldn't want to be taken care of, but she's my mom. It's my duty and my honor to make sure she's good. I'm so glad I got that day to spend with her before her stroke, so I could see her as a friend, as well as my mom.

David Lacks playing guitar

Courtnee Lacks and Erika Johnson

Henrietta Lacks

David and Deborah Lacks

5

WHO'S THE REAL SNAKE

There have been so many people to come in and out of our lives, claiming that they will help the Lacks family. They would come in claiming to care about my grandmother and her legacy. Then, they would promise to help us get the answers that the family deserved. Truthfully, I've lost count of how many crooked people have tried to make money off my grandmother's pain. But, in my opinion, nobody was able to get one over on us the way that Rebecca Skloot did.

Other people have come and gone. They either weren't able to get the payday they wanted, or we figured out what they were really about before they had a chance to do any harm. But Rebecca Skloot was able to come in and execute her plan perfectly. Think about it... She was far from the first person to write about Henrietta Lacks, but she was the only one to make millions of dollars off the story. I need for people to really understand this because it is at the core of my problem with her and that damn book. She came in, hijacked our story, and totally destroyed the whole Lacks family in the process.

The press... HBO... Oprah... they all portray her as some kind of generous and compassionate angel with no other motive but to tell my grandmother's story and expose discrimination in the medical community. But angels don't work for a paycheck, and they especially don't screw other people over just to line their own pockets. That is what Rebecca Skloot did. She benefited from my family's pain and threw us a few crumbs, while her family is financially set for generations to come. Yet, she had the nerve to criticize other people for taking advantage of my family when she did the exact same thing.

One of the people she talked about in the book was a man they referred to as Sir Lord Keenan Kester Cofield. I just know him as Dr. Cofield. He is supposed to be related to Dale's husband's family in some way, but I don't know anything about all of that. I just know that I learned about him through Dale. She said that she was working with him to write a book about Henrietta.

They made Dr. Cofield look really bad in the book and the movie, calling him an "Alabama snake." They made it look like he just came in the door one day and tricked our entire family into trusting and following him. Here we go again with them trying to make us look like a bunch of uneducated, stupid black people who could be easily manipulated by anyone who walked through the door. Now, I will admit that we were far more open to working with a black person than a white person at this point. For years, we had been approached by doctors and lawyers who promised us the world and delivered nothing. So, the family was probably less suspicious of Dr. Cofield, but that doesn't mean that we just handed him our trust the first time he showed up at the door.

Dr. Cofield's entrance into the story happened long before Rebecca Skloot came along. I now know that he was one of the first people to successfully get records and information from Johns Hopkins. Now, he had to go through the courts to get those records, but he got them... and that was something that none of our lawyers had even been able to do before. I don't feel like Dr. Cofield tricked us. Yes, he was talking about filing lawsuits and getting money for the family, but what's wrong with that? At least he was trying to help the family, unlike Rebecca Skloot who was only worried about helping herself. In fact, as far as I'm concerned, she was the snake that came slithering through our family. Not Dr. Cofield.

Dale never told me anything negative about Dr. Cofield. All she ever told us was that she was working with him and a lady named Dr. Wyche to write a book about Henrietta and her cells. Dr. Wyche is a sociologist who was working at Morgan State University at the time. She's a very nice lady. She and another lady named Courtney Speed were working to get recognition for Henrietta in the Turner

Station area, where Henrietta and Day had lived. Speed owned a grocery store in Turner Station, and she was very active in the community. After learning about HeLa and my grandmother, she wanted to build a Henrietta Lacks Museum.

Dr. Wyche started contacting a bunch of government officials and a curator from the Smithsonian. They came to Turner Station and sponsored an event to honor my grandmother. Speed and Dr. Wyche also created the Henrietta Lacks Health History Museum Foundation, Inc. They started selling T-shirts and other paraphernalia to pay for the project, but they never asked any members of the family for permission first. Dale wasn't happy about the situation when she found out. She was tired of everyone *but* the family benefiting financially from our grandmother's name, so she was really suspicious of Speed and Dr. Wyche at first. She eventually came around though when she saw how Dr. Wyche was trying to help get records from Johns Hopkins. She supported the museum project after that. She even asked Dr. Wyche to help her and Dr. Cofield write the book.

Eventually Dr. Wyche was able to get some government recognition for my grandmother when the Maryland State Representative Robert Ehrlich Jr. honored her. She also tried to get the president of Johns Hopkins to acknowledge the hospital's role in the treatment of Henrietta, but the only response she ever got was them saying that they never profited from HeLa cells, which I still don't believe.

Speed went on to create the Henrietta Lacks Legacy Group in Turner Station. It's a nonprofit group and its website says that it "exists to protect, preserve, and promote the legacy of Henrietta Lacks and her contributions to modern medicine (via HeLa Cells) and promote conversations around health equity." Rebecca Skloot wrote that Speed was afraid of Dr. Cofield, but I don't know anything about that. I just know that Dr. Wyche and Dr. Cofield were able to get records from Johns Hopkins that we had never been able to get before.

The Johns Hopkins doctors didn't like working with Dr. Cofield. Here was this persistent black man going in there making accusations and demanding information. I suspect that they didn't like that at all, so they set out to discredit him to Dale. First, they called and told her a lot of negative things about Dr. Cofield, saying that he wasn't a real doctor or lawyer. They called him a fraud and claimed that he had served time in prison. Then, they convinced Dale to sign a document that prevented Johns Hopkins from providing Dr. Cofield with anymore family records. Then, to really get him out of the picture, they called her into a meeting to say that they had this other writer named Rebecca Skloot, and she should work with her. They talked Dale into getting rid of Dr. Wyche and Dr. Cofield to go work with Rebecca Skloot. All of a sudden, they were out of the picture, and that's when everything changed. Johns Hopkins didn't want to deal with the black people who were asking questions, but when the white lady came along, they were suddenly ready and willing to provide information and work with her.

Dr. Cofield filed a lawsuit against Dale, my dad, Courtney Speed, the Henrietta Lacks Health History Museum Foundation, and a bunch of people from Johns Hopkins. Now, I get why this lawsuit made Dale mad, but I think it was more about Johns Hopkins than it was about any member of the Lacks family. Dr. Cofield felt like they were covering up information about my grandmother's death and now they had turned Dale against him too. I still don't think that makes him a snake. This is America. People sue one another all the time. He felt betrayed by the hospital and the family, so he decided to do something about it. I don't like that he sued members of our family, but I don't think that makes him a snake either.

I find it funny that Rebecca Skloot tries to put Dr. Cofield in the same box with the doctors and scientists who took advantage of my family, like she is somehow different. She came in, took our story, inserted herself into it, and claimed it as her own to make millions of dollars. I'm convinced that she painted Dr. Cofield as a villain, so people would focus on him instead of questioning her role or how much she made off of the book. But she is just as guilty in all of this as the doctors who stole my grandmother's DNA, as well as all of those companies and scientists that made money off of it.

In fact, I saw an interview that Rebecca Skloot did at the 2010 Virginia Festival of the Book. The host asked her if

Johns Hopkins willingly worked with her on the book. Here's her response, "Yes, they never tried to hide anything. I had access to all the archives there. This story had been out there in versions for a long time. Little newspaper articles and magazine stories published with just the negatives of the story [saying] woman's cells taken without permission and became an important thing is science. In some ways, I think they were relieved that I was doing the book. [They felt like] great, we can stop answering these questions over and over again from journalists [asking if they had] these cells without permission."

So, the hospital chose her as the person they wanted to deal with. Not the black man who came asking question. Not the black woman who came asking questions. Not even the immediate black family of Henrietta. They wanted to work with someone who came out of nowhere. They helped make her a millionaire while leaving us with nothing.

It wasn't until after Dale's death that Dr. Cofield contacted me. At the time, I didn't know too much about what Dr. Wyche or Dr. Cofield had done. I just knew they had been working with my aunt. But I didn't know how hard they had been fighting to get the true story out about Henrietta's death. Once Johns Hopkins shut it down, they put Henrietta's stuff into a vault to keep people from accessing any of the information. After Dr. Cofield contacted me, I started looking into him more. I found some of his writings about the book and saw that he also thought it was filled with lies and inaccuracies. Dr Cofield was convinced that my grandmother's death was wrongful and the result of medical malpractice, instead of just a progression of the cancer. He says that he has secured documents to support his suspicions, though I have to admit that I have yet to see them.

Here's one of the things he published, "The book by Rebecca Skloot contains a mountain of false to inaccurate alleged notations to statements never made by Dr. Keenan Cofield or others. The book does not address the harms and explain to readers there was not only a misdiagnosis, but a murder [that] took place. Mrs. Henrietta Lacks was murdered at Hopkins. When you don't have a medical license, and your treatment plan causes the patient's death, that is murder. The whole entire book to movie is a sham and scam by Rebecca Skloot, Oprah to HBO, that includes Johns Hopkins Hospital and University."

Dr. Cofield told me that doctors treating my grandmother didn't have proper licenses. He said that was the reason for her misdiagnosis, and her ultimate death. He calls it negligent homicide and said that we could have legal grounds to sue the hospital because there's no statute of limitations on homicide. I don't know if his allegations are true, but with all of the secrecy and lies around my grandmother's death, I am more than willing to hear him out. Plus, the medical profession has been mistreating black people for decades, experimenting on us and withholding necessary treatments. I don't put anything past those doctors, especially back then. They saw my grand-mother as an uneducated black woman who had no voice to advocate for herself or even question what they were doing to her body. So, there's no telling what they actually did to her.

Rebecca Skloot tries to paint Dr. Cofield like a crazy person in the book. I can't label him as crazy though. The info he has… he hasn't given it to me yet. He says he will, but he hasn't yet. Who knows though? Maybe it's informa-tion that he considers important and he doesn't want to send it through e-mail. I'm just neutral on this. I'm not going to judge the man. I'll just wait for the evidence and let it speak for itself. I don't know what documents he has for sure, and I don't know what he can or can't prove. What I *do* know is that when I look down the list of the people who benefited financially from my family and my grand-mother, his name isn't there. I could decide that he is a bad guy based on what Rebecca Skloot wrote about him, but knowing all the other lies she told, why would I take her word over his?

Bobbette, Lawrence Lacks Jr., and Alfred Carter

Deborah (Dale) Lacks and children

Ronnie and Donnie – our nicknames

Church in Clover Virginia

6

SKLOOT ENTERS THE PICTURE

When Rebecca Skloot was first brought to our attention, none of us trusted her. In fact, we didn't even want to meet her. She has even said in interview after interview that it took more than a year and a half for Dale to come around to helping her. Here's one of the quotes that I found, "January 1, 2000 when I first met the family. It took about a year and a half to get them to meet me. They didn't know who to trust. They were understandably weary of me." She got that part right. We were all very weary of her. By that time, we had dealt with so many fraudulent people that we weren't trying to deal with anyone new. We just knew that there was a woman trying to speak with the family about Henrietta's cells.

From what she said in the book, Rebecca Skloot's first introduction came through Dr. Ronald Pattillo, a black researcher who worked under Dr. Gey in studying Henrietta's cells. The family met him while he was working at the Morehouse School of Medicine in Atlanta, Georgia. This was long before the book came out. He held conferences at the school in honor of my grandmother and he invited some of the family members down to speak. I'm not sure what exactly took place after he made the introduction between Rebecca Skloot and Dale. I know it was around the time when Dale was talking about writing her own book though.

From what I understand, Dale finally agreed to speak with Rebecca Skloot after Johns Hopkins called Dale in for a meeting and advised her to work with Rebecca Skloot. Dale thought that their approval would mean that she could get access to more information from the hospital, which turned out to be true. But other members of the family felt that a Johns Hopkins approval made Rebecca Skloot even more suspect and untrustworthy.

She tried hard to get Dale on her side though. When Dale refused to speak with her, she called Sonny about meeting the family. He ignored her a few times before getting that first meeting together at my mom's house. I really hate the way Rebecca Skloot described this meeting in her book and the way it played out in the movie. For one thing, she had my dad cooking in the kitchen, and wiping his hands on his T-shirt, which had to be an absolute lie. My dad never cooked. My mom did all the cooking. That's just another example of how she replaced the truth with whatever fiction she wanted to add. Then, I feel like she tried to put a negative spin on the fact that Dale told her to speak with the men of the family first, but this was the dynamic of our family.

My dad took care of everyone and he took the protection of his family and his mother's memory very seriously. Plus, if it was a male ego thing, why was my mother present? Having her talk to Day, my dad, Sonny and my mom was just an extension of the way my family operated—at least before Rebecca Skloot came along. They were not trying to hurt or oppress Dale. They were trying to protect her and the entire family. Remember, my mom helped to raise Dale into adulthood. When she got into trouble, my parents helped her out. When she became pregnant unexpectedly, my mom encouraged her to stay in school. They always had Dale's best interest in mind. Plus, my dad knew how troubled and upset Dale was about the cells and he didn't want anyone bringing anymore pain into her life. In the movie, after Dale tells Rebecca Skloot to talk to the men, she says "I don't want to be hurt no more." I think that was done to try and make my father and uncle look bad, like they were the ones hurting Dale. But in reality, me, dad, and Sonny were trying to keep Dale from being hurt by Rebecca Skloot. They didn't want to let a snake into the family or into Dale's life, but unfortunately, that's exactly what ended up happening.

I knew that Dale had started working with Rebecca Skloot to write a book, but I didn't have many of the details about what was going on during that time. I didn't really get back into the picture until Dale came to me and voiced her dissatisfaction with Rebecca Skloot. She was disappointed in how she was handling the partnership of the book. It's no secret that Dale always felt that the family should have been compensated for the contributions of Henrietta. It's also no secret that Dale was a business-minded woman who knew the value of the Lacks story. Contrary to what Rebecca Skloot and Gayle King may think, Dale wasn't some crazy irrational woman. She went to school for a lot of things, like cosmetology. She and her second husband even opened up a church in Dundalk. She knew what the Lacks story was worth and there is no way that she was going along with being cut out of those profits.

Rebecca Skloot tried to make her look like some crazy lady, clueless to everything in her life—almost like a helpless child. But that's not who Dale was. She knew very well that the Lacks family should have financially benefited from the story, and when she found out that it wasn't going to happen, she was angry about it. I read one article that quoted her as saying, "We never knew they took her cells, and people done got filthy rich [from HeLa-based research], but we don't get a dime." About Johns Hopkins, she said, "all they do is pat me on my shoulder and put me out the door. Hopkins, they don't care." That's why I halfway believe that part in the book where Dale was questioning Rebecca Skloot about the money she was getting. That sounds like Dale and it goes along with the concerns she was voicing to me. She was always suspicious of Rebecca Skloot making money off of the family.

From what Dale told me, she found out that Rebecca Skloot wasn't going to split the book proceeds with the family. Instead, she was only going to set up a foundation in the family's name—a foundation that she would control. That's another lie from the book. Rebecca Skloot made it look like Dale was happy and satisfied with the foundation, but she wasn't. She wanted the family to directly benefit from the book, which she thought was going to happen the whole time she was working with Rebecca Skloot.

When Dale finally saw through her bullshit and realized what she was really up to, she was not OK with it. Rebecca Skloot conveniently left that part out of the book though. Instead, she focused on trying to make herself look like a martyr…. like she was sacrificing something for the benefit of the Lacks family. She went out of her way to try and show how financially strapped she was while writing the book, talking about all of her bills and her broken down car. Yeah, she may have been struggling then, but she is a millionaire now—off of my grandmother's legacy. She wants people to forget about how much money she made, so she tries to portray herself as some kind of crusader, only concerned with telling the truth about Henrietta Lacks. But Rebecca Skloot was only concerned with making money off of our family and keeping us out of the benefits.

She wants people to see Dale as this abusive woman who she was gracious enough to put up with, but I don't believe any of it. Like I said before, so much of that book was fiction. It's almost impossible to figure out what's real and what she made up for her own benefit. Then Rebecca Skloot tries to act like inserting herself into the book was Dale's idea. How convenient is that? You're a journalist and from what I've read, journalists aren't supposed to insert themselves into the story. That's simple Journalism 101. She did it though, making the story about herself so she could spin it and present it to make her look good and the Lacks family look terrible... and then she tries to say it was all Dale's idea.

Once Dale stopped working with Rebecca Skloot, she came to us and told us about their falling out. She told us how she was planning to cut us out of any proceeds from the book. Having found that out, she didn't want anything else to do with Rebecca Skloot. She cut off ties with her and stopped contributing to the book. Rebecca Skloot doesn't write about any of that though, conveniently leaving that part out of the story.

Dale went to her deathbed upset about Rebecca Skloot and the book. She hated the fact that the family wouldn't get any financial benefit from it. I was living in Dale's apartment in the month or so before her death, while she was in the rehabilitation center. She had become extremely depressed, which I believe had a lot to do with her relationship with Rebecca Skloot. On her discharge day, I went to pick her up from the center and took her home. She looked so good, better than I had seen her look in years. She was actually glowing. Dale thanked me for taking care of the house and walked around commenting on how well I had cleaned it. It was so good seeing her. I didn't stay too long because I wanted her to get settled in. In hindsight, I wish I had stayed there with her though.

One week later, Sonny called and said that Dale wasn't answering the phone. He'd been calling and calling, but still no answer. When he went over to check on her, Dale was laying on the bed fully clothed with her coat and hat on. He said it looked like she was going to meet somebody. She was laying there dead with her hands crossed over her chest. So, I'm thinking to myself, "Who gets fully dressed in a coat and hat and then lies down on the bed to die?" It just seemed awfully strange to me. They didn't do an autopsy on her to find out the cause of death. A lot of the family wished they had done one though, because we had a lot of suspicions. I'm not accusing anyone of anything, but once you start talking about being cut out of million-dollar deals... it was all just very suspicious to some of us.

A while after Dale's death, Rebecca Skloot came to the house with a transcript of the book for the family to read. We were cooking out as usual, and everyone was in the backyard. Me, my mom, and my dad read it. I'm not sure who else read through it at that time. After looking over the transcript, my dad called Rebecca Skloot to the side and told her that he was unhappy with the book and how it portrayed the family. He didn't like that the family was made to look poor and uneducated, when that was far from the truth. He told her that she needed to take some of the untrue things out, like my grandmother being illiterate. She told him no to changing the book because it was her story. Now, how did this book change from Henrietta's story to Dale's story to Rebecca Skloot's story?

I believe she put this narrative out into the world to benefit herself. There's a video of Rebecca Skloot talking about the book on C-SPAN in 2010. When asked who Henrietta Lacks was, the first words out of her mouth were "a poor African American tobacco farmer." This is the picture of the Lacks family that she wanted America to see. A black woman who made such an important contribution to the world—for them to highlight the negative about her family instead of portraying us with kindness and in a good light, it was one more stab in an ongoing act to destroy the Lacks family legacy. It just didn't stop, from getting permission to do the movie and book... to talking with her estate. Rebecca Skloot knew that dividing the family was key to getting that book out. We've seen it happen plenty of times. A person comes in to advocate for a situation that affects a black family, and instead of telling the whole story, they split the family and tell the side that makes their story more entertaining and agreeable to readers.

After getting nowhere with Rebecca Skloot about his concerns, my dad voiced his worries to the family. He told them that he wasn't happy with the way the family was being portrayed. He also pointed out that the family wouldn't be getting any money from the proceeds of the book. I will never forget that day. We started the cookout as a big united family, but by the end of the night, we were starting to split over this book that Rebecca Skloot had written. As I said before, my dad was the patriarch of the family. Even while Day was alive, everyone deferred to my dad for guidance. Now, here he was trying to offer what he felt was in the best interest of the family; yet, they were more concerned with the fame and fortune that they thought they were going to get (which didn't happen), rather than giving a true and accurate reflection of our family. Here's another one of Rebecca's quotes, "Multibillion-dollar industries were born out of these cells. Yet they can't afford health insurance. They are quite poor." It was a narrative that she just kept repeating over and over... and one that the public unfortunately believed.

Again, I go back to the fact that she calls herself a journalist. In one interview she even spoke about the impact that journalists have on the people they write about. She claimed to have considered what her ethical duties were to the Lacks family as a writer. She said, "I thought about being another person who was coming along and potentially benefiting from this in ways they might not. So, I thought about ways to make sure it benefited them if it was going to benefit me. So, the foundation was one of the first things I wanted to do. I saw how traumatized they were and wanted to approach it in a way that didn't damage them further." I'll get back to the so-called foundation later. She decided that, in order to write this book and make it a success, she had to make our family as unapproachable as possible. Even if you only read a small part of the book, you will see that she tried not to write anything positive about the family. She went out of her way to make Dale and the rest of us look bad, so she could sell more books. And again, what does any of that have to do with my grandmother's cells? She claimed to be so concerned about getting Henrietta's story out. She could have done that without dragging our family's reputation through the mud.

Another problem I have with Rebecca Skloot is that she never returned our precious family photographs. I don't even know for sure how she got them, but she has admitted to having our family pictures while she was writing the book. She told my dad that she would mail them to him, but she never did. We never gave Rebecca Skloot any pictures or permission to use or publish any of our private family photos. That picture from the cover of the book... it's been published all over the internet. But it was used without permission. My dad felt that there must be some type of copyright infringement involved, but when he tried to seek legal help, no lawyers would help him. We have asked for our family photos back repeatedly. In fact, I have no clue where any of the pictures are now. I just know they aren't where they are supposed to be. Our family pictures are so important to me, especially with the family so divided now. It made me and my dad smile to look at those pictures and reminisce, but even that part of our family history had been taken from us.

After the book came out, my father started voicing his concerns publicly. All of the attention around his mother made him sad in some ways, but empowered in others. Like I said before, the pain of watching his mother die was a lot for my dad to deal with, so he suppressed a lot of those memories and refused to speak about them. But once the book came out, his pride and desire for the truth began to outweigh his unwillingness to speak about it. He started talking to me about inaccuracies within the book. He even started sharing some of his memories about his mother with me, telling me stories and using real-life examples to argue against things Rebecca Skloot had written in the book.

I feel like this is a good time to give a broader picture of my dad. While he loved and adored his mother very much, he could also be a hardhead. He used to tell me about leaving the house when his mother was out and sneaking down to the water to dive off a pier and swim the channel. He said his mother would get so mad, tearing his behind up when she found out. He didn't care though. Every chance he got, he would sneak out and go down to that pier. That's why my dad is such a good swimmer to this day, and he made sure that I could also swim at an early age.

My dad is a fixer. If something is wrong, he wants to find the solution and fix it. Now, he may not finish every-thing he starts fixing, but he will at least put in the effort.

I remember how he would start on all of these different projects, but never finish them. Like the way he put paneling up in my mom's house but didn't finish the molding around the walls. He would get so excited about a new project, and he fully intended to finish each one, but it just never happened.

When I was about thirteen years old, my father came home with a minibike in the back of his truck. I was as happy as I don't know what. My mom was upset, yelling at my dad, "Why did you get that boy a minibike? He's going to kill himself!" Neither one of us paid her much mind though. Instead, we took the minibike off the truck and cranked it up. When it started, the engine noise cracked the air... but the noise was all I got. The minibike that I was so excited to get wouldn't move an inch. The engine revved and revved when you pressed on the clutch, but it just would not move. I know that made my mom happy. Yeah, I got a bike, but the joke was on me because I couldn't ride it.

My friends and I found a way to make it work though—at least for a couple of days. We had an alley behind our house on Kitmore Road, and it had a little downslope. We would jump on the bike, crank it up, and then drift downhill. We thought we were doing something, making all of that noise. But all we were really doing was drifting down the hill. It was still cool though, until we had to take on the backbreaking deed of pushing that heavy bike back up the hill. It didn't take long for us to grow tired of that broken minibike.

Another story about my dad happened when I was much older. After graduating from high school, I enlisted in the army. My family was so proud of me, but especially my dad. He had served in the military and now his oldest son was following in his footsteps. I was stationed in Germany, where I spent two years. My main focus in the military was cooking. I loved to cook, but I started to have trouble with my feet. It got too unbearable to stand in the kitchen cooking all day, and after two years of service, I received an honorable discharge. I tried to cook in a couple of local restaurants after returning to Baltimore, but the same problems with my feet kept me from work. That's when I started driving trucks. I did that for many years before going to work in my parents' corner market. Their market did quite well. I worked there for years and it was there that I met my wife and we have been together ever since.

With the market bringing in some real money, my father decided to buy a big 35-foot boat. It was a nice boat with a bunch of upgrades. I wanted to remodel it though, to make it look jazzier because the whole interior was dripping in red, white, and blue. My pops had to fix the boat's engine. I didn't have much faith that he would get it done because… here we go with another engine problem, but he did eventually fix it. I hadn't gone to school to learn how to be seaworthy, but my friends and I would go down to the boathouse and fish right off of the docked boat. We never took the boat out one time, but that didn't bother us. We were just going down to the dock and fishing.

Eventually, my father got disenchanted with the boat and didn't want it anymore. He told me and my friends that we could have it as long as we paid the docking fees of $100 a month. We decided to all chip in and really fix the boat up, so we could do something adventurous with it. We were so excited talking about our plans for the boat, but they never happened. Even to this day, my friends and I talk about it and feel sorry that we didn't take advantage of that opportunity my dad gave us. I mean, most people never even get a chance to board a boat like that. It had a kitchen, bathroom, upper and lower deck. It was just a really nice boat. I think my father wound up selling it. I wish I had taken advantage of that. I didn't want to go way out in the water, but I would have liked to go up to the New York harbor or somewhere.

We missed out on a great adventure, but this is just one example of the many opportunities that my father presented to my family. Rebecca Skloot tried hard to paint him as an ignorant, selfish man, but my dad made a lot of sacrifices to elevate our family to a good life.

David Lacks (Courtesy of Joyce Foster)

Henrietta Lacks' family

Lawrence and Bobbette Lacks

Bobbette Lacks

7

HBO AND OPRAH COME KNOCKING

I can't recall when Oprah Winfrey actually bought the rights to Rebecca Skloot's book. I just remember hearing about it one day. It was exciting for someone as famous as Oprah to be interested in our grandmother's story. Knowing her background as an investigative journalist, I hoped that she might seek out the true Lacks family story and expose Rebecca Skloot's lies. Back then, I saw the movie deal as an opportunity to right a wrong. I know better now though.

There was a lot going on during that time, with HBO and Oprah's involvement. For one thing, this is when some of the family members decided to completely sell us all out, for just $16,000. HBO offered us the opportunity to serve as consultants on the film. When I say "us," I mean my dad, Sonny, Abdul, Jeri Lacks, Alfred Carter Jr., and La Tonya Carter (Dale's children). They sent over a contract that said how much each person would be paid and included all of these rules we had to follow as consultants. My dad was dealing with a lawyer who advised him not to speak with Oprah or sign the agreement. At the time, I didn't know all that the agreement entailed, but I thought that my dad should at least have a one-on-one conversation with Oprah before making a final decision. My mother agreed with me. We all told him he should talk to her because we felt that he could have gotten in front of the story with Oprah before the movie came out. We all figured that he may have been able to negotiate better terms by speaking with her and discussing his concerns.

Since my dad refused to talk to her, the HBO people started communicating with me directly in hopes that I would bring my father around. Regarding me specifically, the contract said: "HBO wishes to consult directly with Artist, Ron Lacks, Artist's son, shall be authorized to speak for Artist and shall be the conduit between HBO and Artist."

The amount of compensation for consulting was $16,667.67.

That part of the contract stated:

"Artist shall accept:

(k) The aggregate amount of Sixteen Thousand Six Hundred Sixty-six and 67/100 Dollars ($16,666.67) (the "Consultant Fee"), which shall be payable as follows:

(i)   Fifty percent (50%) promptly following delivery to HBO of this executed and notarized Certificate of Engagement; and

(ii) Fifty percent (50%) promptly following the later of (A) commencement of principal photography of the Project, (B) completion of Artist's Consulting Services as reasonably required by HBO, and (C) eighteen months from the date that a fully- executed copy of this Agreement is delivered to HBO."

My father and Sonny met right here at my house to discuss the contract. We all discussed the pros and cons of the contract and the money being offered. Dale's children weren't present for the conversation, which wasn't a surprise. I doubt that HBO ever had any problem getting them to sign off. It seems like they have never had a bit of hesitation when it came to selling out the family. Rebecca Skloot knew that she needed an ally within the family. She also knew that my dad was not going to be that person. So, she needed someone she could control and use to give her some credibility. Jeri Lacks, Sonny's daughter, became that person, and she still is to this day. She was hand-selected by Rebecca Skloot and HBO to be the Lacks family representative. The contract even named her as the go-to person: "for expediency (a) HBO shall be entitled to designate, and has designated, one Lacks Family member (Jeri Lacks) as the point person for the Lacks Consultants (the 'Point Person')."

Sitting at my dining table, my dad and Sonny went back and forth about the contact. My dad felt that the money being offered for the Lacks family story was a very low bar. I remember him saying, "I've seen Oprah give out cars on her TV show worth more than that." He also took issue with the amount of control HBO would have over the story. My dad was finally fully aware of how important my grandmother's contributions had been to science and he wasn't comfortable giving some outsiders free will over how they wanted to use it. Sonny's argument was that we'd been going through the drama of the book for years with no compensation. At least the HBO deal would give the family some money.

My dad and Sonny went back and forth for a while before my dad decided that he would not sign the agreement and Sonny decided that he would sign it. Though he voiced his opinion, my dad never tried to block anyone from doing anything. He knew everybody had to make their own choice about the contract, but he stood by his decision not to sign it... and after looking over the entire agreement and listening to all the arguments, I agreed with him. The amount was too small, and no amount of money was worth selling out the Lacks family legacy. I believe that, because my dad refused to sign, they made him one of the least relevant characters in the whole movie, even though he was the one with the clearest memory of my grandmother and the executor of my grandmother's estate. How can you tell the story of a woman's life without any input from the only immediate family member with any real memories of her? It just didn't make any sense.

A little while later, Oprah came here to Baltimore to meet the family and take pictures. I had a hard time finding someone to watch my mom, so I arrived about fifteen minutes late. By that time, they had already taken the photos. My wife and I missed the family pictures, but we were able to take a photo with Oprah by ourselves later that afternoon. When we first walked in, all eyes were on us. I think Rebecca Skloot had built me up to be some kind of boogieman. You can just tell when you walk into a room and all eyes are on you. You can just feel the awkwardness. So, Oprah walked over to me and I think the words she used were "I've heard a lot about you." I politely told her that I wasn't a troublemaker. I just wanted to get the story straight. I told her how important Henrietta's legacy was to me and my family. It was a story that would go down in history.

I told Oprah that my dad and I just wanted to let her know about some of the things in the book we didn't agree with. That's when she told me that they weren't strictly going by everything Rebecca Skloot put in the book. She said they may change things when they felt it was appropriate. The movie director told me the same thing. I thanked Oprah for her assurance and told her that I appreciated her. I suggested a sit down to discuss some of the things in the book that were wrong, if not straight out lies about the family, but I never spoke with her again and never got a chance to tell her anything more. I would have liked to tell her about some of the accomplishments and good times the family had that were not in the book. I wanted Oprah to see that Rebecca Skloot only focused on the negative, including very little positive facts about the Lacks family and how we were raised.

I wanted her to know that we grew up as middle-class citizens. I wanted her to know that Day and my parents had good jobs. They weren't worried about paying rent or where our next meal was coming from. Even my Aunt Dale talked about this in one of her interviews before her death, saying, "We weren't poor. We were living comfortably." Our family never felt poor even though Rebecca Skloot portrayed us that way in the book. In fact, I never knew I was poor until I read the book.

That was the last time I ever spoke to Oprah. She actually talked about our meeting in an interview later on. She said, "His son, Ron, spoke to me at the luncheon that we held and said to me then that he didn't appreciate the way Rebecca had portrayed their family as being poor people, and that they weren't poor. I said to him, 'That's not my interpretation of the story. I interpreted it as you were working class, middle class, and certainly people striving to make a living every day.'" I get where she's coming from, but Oprah saw it that way because, once again, she is seeing it from the perspective of a black family only a few generations out of slavery. But a lot, if not most, of the people reading the book don't share that perspective.

They don't understand the dynamics of our family history and they do not see us in that light. I know this to be true because I constantly hear us referred to as a "poor black family" in interviews of Rebecca Skloot and other so-called "experts" on our family.

My dad's decision not to sign the consulting agreement also became news for the press. *The Washington Post* reported that he "turned down HBO's offer of a $16,000 consultant fee on the project and refused an advance screening because he was asked 'to sign my rights away. I wouldn't be allowed to talk about my mother anymore.'" My dad's lawyer had advised him that some parts of contract forbid him from speaking out against the project or any of its contents. Having already dealt with the lies of the book, we weren't willing to give up our rights to speak out in support of our family, even if it meant speaking against the book and movie. For some family members, $16,000 was enough for them to keep quiet in support of the lies being told about our family, but our legacy meant way too much to my dad and me.

Oprah said that she was disappointed by my dad's remarks. She said, "Lawrence Lacks was offered multiple opportunities to participate as a consultant on this film, along with the rest of the family members and each time, (HBO) was turned down." Yes, the offer was made, but not nearly enough money was offered, and the terms were completely one-sided against us.

I never felt any negativity about Oprah's part in all this. Even after the movie came out, I didn't have any ill feelings against her. My dad turned down the invite to talk with her when the book first came out, because his lawyer at the time told him not to. We knew then that it was a big mistake, so I can't hold her totally responsible for everything that happened. I get that it was a good opportunity for Oprah, and to bring public attention to everything that Henrietta had done. I still feel that it was a great thing for her and HBO to get behind. I just wish she had sent her own investigators out to learn the truth instead of taking Rebecca Skloot's word for it. I feel like she was duped by Rebecca Skloot too. I believed Oprah when she said that she wouldn't simply take Rebecca Skloot's description of everything, but that didn't happen. I still had no bad feelings against her though... until I saw her on national TV with Gayle King, laughing and disrespecting my deceased aunt.

Another part of the drama around the HBO movie was a PR agent that my dad and I hired, named Karen Campbell. She was short and a bit chubby, loud, and filled with energy. We went down to this lawyer's office that wanted to pick up our case and the PR lady she wanted us to meet was not there, so she got us to meet Karen instead. We were sitting at the meeting and Karen was really selling herself, talking about all of the positive stuff she could do to help us and get our story out to the public. My dad and I were really impressed with her, but I don't think the lawyer felt that way. About a day or two later, Karen started calling us and somehow convinced us to get rid of the lawyer.

I know it sounds crazy, but she was just saying things that we had never heard said before, about what she could do and how she could get it to all come together. She really wowed and convinced us. We liked what she was saying and how she was saying it. She blasted out a news release denouncing the "inaccurate" and "racist" portrayal of the Lacks family. She even got us interviews on TV and radio, which no one ever did before. She was aggressive and we kind of liked that. But in hindsight, I know she was too aggressive in her tactics and burned a lot of bridges for us.

First, she sent out emails demanding that the Henrietta Lacks Foundation, set up by Rebecca Skloot, be transferred to my dad's control. I didn't have a problem with that one because I don't trust Rebecca Skloot and I never liked the idea of her having control of the foundation in the first place. Then, she started contacting HBO and Oprah's production company to demand that they each donate millions of dollars to the foundation. Now, this one she did on her own. In fact, we didn't even know about it until after she'd sent those emails. She also sent letters to the speaker's agency about which family members were being allowed to speak at events and requested a large advance from a publishing company for us to write our own book.

I have to admit that Karen wasn't making my dad and I look good with some of her crazy demands... but like I said, she did do a good job at getting us some press time before we ended our contract with her. My dad and I had interviews on TV, the radio, and in national publications.

While a lot of the major outlets tried to paint us as bitter or unjustified in our concerns, some of the smaller black publications took us seriously and did a good job at getting our side of the story out there. What's interesting, though, is that, in preparation for writing this book, I tried to find a lot of those articles on the internet, and almost every one of them was either removed or inaccessible. It's as if our objections to the book and movie have been completely wiped away. Makes me wonder...

As my dad and I became more vocal about the situation, some of the family members came out in support of the book and the movie. *The Baltimore Sun* published their official statement, which said, "The Lacks family is a large and diverse group whose members have distinct opinions, but we are all entitled to speak publicly about our family's legacy and our individual experiences. We will continue to spread our positive message to schools, libraries, associations, and community organizations worldwide, ensuring that Henrietta Lacks' contributions to humanity are never forgotten." It was signed by Sonny, a couple of grandchildren, great-grandchildren, and a daughter-in-law of my grandmother.

Oprah spoke out about the family split, saying that HBO was "just trying to do a film to bring the story to light." She called the controversy "a family disagreement that I would be happy not to be in the middle of." I hate that Rebecca Skloot was able to come into our family and cause so much tension between us, but I don't regret speaking up for our family's reputation. There's no amount of money that would make me tell lies about the Lacks family or paint them in a negative view.

Courtnee Lacks Brown

Lawrence and Ron Lacks

Marriage Certificate showing Henrietta Lacks' cursive signature

Lawrence Lacks Jr. and Lisa Lacks

8

THE AFTERMATH

Our family dynamic has changed dramatically since the release of the book and movie. The tight knit family that spent weekends and holidays together is now splintered down the middle. On one side are the ones who support the book and speak out in favor of it. My parents and I stand pretty much alone on the other side, determined to speak the truth about the Lacks family.

To promote the book, Rebecca Skloot and the publishing company started scheduling members of the family to attend speaking engagements, which really deepened the divide. I was invited to participate in one of the first events. It was set up by Jeri and we went to speak at Clarksville University. Jeri had become kind of a manager over all of the speaking engagements. She would decide who could speak and who couldn't. Like I said before,

Rebecca Skloot has Jeri under her control. She trusts her not to speak out against the book, even about the stuff that's clearly untrue.

So, she made Jeri the gatekeeper of all the speaking engagements.

I think Rebecca Skloot has real contempt for the Lacks family. She didn't want to have anything to do with us. She didn't want the family to have equal booking at speaking engagements. There were even times when the family was denied out-of-town hotel accommodations, while she was given a great big suite. I know Jeri gets paid for speaking engagements, but I don't know how much or when. But she controls a lot of what the family says and does when it comes to the book and movie, and if our family pictures ever got sent back, I guarantee they were sent to Jeri instead of the original owners.

It was just me and Sonny at this Clarksville engagement. We went up the night before and had dinner with some of the school officials. While we were eating, some of them started asking me for my opinion about the book. Well, I wasn't about to lie, so I voiced my concerns. Many of them actually seemed pleased that I was going to present another perspective on the book. The next day, we went to speak. There were a lot of people there. In fact, it was so crowded that they had to open an overflow room. Sonny and I sat on the panel with the interviewer. When they asked if we shared in any profits from the book, I told them that we did not get even a half a cent from the book and how Dale had stopped working with Rebecca Skloot after learning that we weren't going to share in the profits. I also told the audience that I disagree with how they characterized my family in the book.

After the interview, we mingled with the audience and several people voiced their concerns about us not making any money from the book. A lot of people assume that we get royalties or something from the book or movie, but we don't, and they are always surprised to hear that. In fact, throughout this entire process, people are always shocked that Rebecca Skloot was not sharing the book profits with the family. Partly because she always presented herself as if she was looking out for the Lacks family, but she really wasn't. After the event, Jeri told me that I wasn't invited back anymore and that I would not be invited to anymore events. Sonny was invited back though. He hadn't said anything negative about the book in public, even though he had plenty to say when we were in private, so he was welcome at all of the speaking engagements going forward. In fact, he kept taking part in them up until he had a stroke. They also don't invite Abdul to go and speak. They never knew what he might say, so they just didn't invite him.

They stopped inviting my mom after her one and only appearance. She was understandably upset about how she was portrayed in the book. She didn't like the way most of the family members were portrayed in the book, especially Day. Like I said, my mom and Day were very close, and she resented the way they tried to make him out to be a villain… even accusing him of giving Henrietta syphilis. After she spoke out about it at an event, she was never invited to speak again.

The only family members that had no problem with the way the family was portrayed were the ones who were paid to like it. I would ask them, "How can you go out there and promote a book when they are writing negative things about your family?" They would always respond that Dale gave Rebecca Skloot all of the information she used. But how do they know? Dale is not here to back up Rebecca Skloot's story. So, why are they taking the word of this opportunistic woman as if it's the God's honest truth? If you look at the speaking events, it is always the same crew. I have inquired about speaking in recent years, but Jeri flat out told me that I'm not invited because I don't speak in favor of the book. Jeri said that if I wanted to speak, I'd have to get my own platform.

We aren't even sure if some of the people they invite to do these speaking events are really even related to us. I have known Toni for a long time. We used to live a couple of doors down from her family on Biddle Street when I was growing up. I always knew Toni as Williams Wooden's daughter. It wasn't until years later that it was told to my mother that she was my father's daughter. It was the beginning of a really hard time for my family. By that time, my mother had had enough of my father's infidelity. That's when their marriage went downhill. Though we went back and forth about the issue of Toni's paternity, there was no

DNA test for her to take back then. So, we all just accepted Toni as part of the family. But she wanted to know the truth, so, in 2010, she decided to take a DNA test. Sonny and I tried to persuade her not to do it. She was our family and we felt that she should just leave it alone, but she couldn't and now we all know that she is not my father's biological child.

I still consider Toni to be my sister. She's always been a very loving person and I'm glad to have gotten to know her throughout the years. The love that she has shown to this family is undeniable. I could always go to Toni's house for a visit, and I would feel at home because that's the type of person she is, and I love her to this day. I'm also grateful to Toni for not getting involved with Rebecca Skloot and her BS. Toni never injected her beliefs on how the family should be feeling about the book. But unfortunately, one of Toni's daughters—even after the DNA test proved that my dad wasn't Toni's father—continues to put herself out there on speaking tours, presenting herself as Henrietta Lacks granddaughter. And to this day, she still refuses to stop interfering in the Lacks family story. That's the reason why I felt the need to speak about the issue of paternity. I wasn't trying to hurt Toni, but the truth needed to be told. Her daughters are not the granddaughters of Henrietta Lacks and it pisses me off to see this lie continuously put out there as the truth.

For me, it's about the way that they stripped away my father's leadership of the family. It wasn't until the Henrietta story came out that all of these distant family members started coming around, and because they were willing to go along with the lies, they were welcomed and pushed to the front. My dad has been the head of the family for years and when he told them he didn't want them going out and speaking on behalf of the family, he felt betrayed because they didn't listen. They were not immediate family to be making decisions about the Lacks family, and that is what my dad was trying to explain to them. Just because he had an outside child (if she is actually even his), that doesn't give that child or any of that child's children the right to come in and speak for the Lacks family as a whole.

Things were poorly done, and things were said in anger, but my father was losing total control of the family. He was depressed for a long time. Jeri took the family into a totally different direction. If she said it was OK, it was OK. Disregard what Lawrence was saying.

Though we weren't welcome at the family speaking engagements, I was invited to speak at one really wonderful event. My wife got a direct email from Tuskegee Institute. I had done a couple of radio shows—one with the Morgan State University station and one with other station where we were allowed to speak the truth. Somebody from Tuskegee heard the interview, and they emailed me and my wife to find out the story behind it. We were so used to being left out of speaking engagements that my wife thought it was a prank at first. Once we learned that it was real, we called them back and found out that they truly wanted us to come speak. They sent us hotel and transportation information and everything. When we got there, they gave us a tour of the campus and showed us how Henrietta's cells were being used. It was such a beautiful experience. We felt appreciated and welcome to speak our minds. Even the mayor of the city was there. It was a very big event.

The audience was so open to us. They wanted to hear what the Lacks family had to say on both sides. We also talked a lot about how researchers tried to hide the fact that her cells are used for so many different things. At first, it was really strange for me. Speaking publicly is new to me, but I tried to fill that role. It needed to be done and somebody needed to speak out.

After I spoke, people were coming up and greeting me. They told me how pleased they were that I told them things that they had no idea about, like other facts from our family history and our disappointment with Rebecca Skloot's book. They had no idea that some members of the Lacks family felt that way. My mom's stroke happened while my wife and I were at Tuskegee, so several of our hosts knew what was going on. They showed so much concern for her and her condition. It was a really great event that turned out to be an amazing experience for me and my wife.

Rebecca Skloot and Jeri were also sure to keep me and my dad out of the National Institutes of Health (NIH) deal. That whole situation started in 2013 when some German scientists published an article comparing DNA from the HeLa cell lines with healthy human cells. They put our family's private medical information right out in the public for everyone to see. Once the family learned about the article, we voiced our concerns about the violation of our privacy. Rebecca Skloot worked out a meeting between the NIH and certain members of the family to address the issues. Once again, the black family's concern was not important enough to make things happen, but once the white lady got involved, the highest medical organization in the country became willing to sit down and negotiate.

They came up with a program where scientists have to put in an application before they can access the DNA data of my grandmother's cells. Then a board—including two members of the Lacks family—looks over the application and decides whether to approve it or not. When they announced the program, NIH representatives said, "The understanding reached with the Lacks family respects their wishes to enable scientific progress while ensuring public acknowledgement of the enormous contribution made by the late Henrietta Lacks. In addition, the understanding gives the Lacks family a seat at the table in reviewing applications for controlled access to Henrietta Lacks' whole genome data."

Not one of my father's children was even offered an opportunity to represent the family on the NIH board. Once again, we were purposely left out of decisions involving my grandmother's cells. I wasn't surprised though. I already knew something was up when Rebecca Skloot got involved with the deal. Most writers will write a book and move on to something else, but not Rebecca Skloot! She wasn't going anywhere. She made it her goal to stay involved in the Lacks family for life.

I remember reading a 2013 interview that she did in a magazine called *The Scientist*. The article said that Rebecca Skloot was "instrumental in bringing... researchers and bioethicists to the table to hammer out the deal." She obviously knew the key players that she wanted at the NIH meetings. In the article, she said, "I talked to Francis Collins and Kathy Hudson at the NIH as sources when I was writing about the genome. So, when I first started talking to them it was to interview them about the fact that this genome had been published without consent. And then we just sort of started talking about what happens next. So, I said, 'OK, how about we get everybody in a room?'" Then, she claimed to bring in other people who knew our family and who we supposedly trusted. She said, "I sort of felt like I wasn't going to be involved. And then the family said, 'Oh no you're not!' So, they really wanted me to be there." What she conveniently left out was the fact that my father and I specifically asked that she not be on the phone during the meeting. I told her right then that this was a family matter and not her concern. We also had a lawyer at that meeting, but I can't even remember his name because he quickly removed himself from the situation after finding out that Jeri and the other family members were going against the wishes of my dad, even though they knew that my father was the executor of his mother's estate.

When my dad objected to Rebecca Skloot's partici-
pation by phone, her response to him was, "Jeri said that
I could be here." By this time, I was pissed the hell off! Jeri
and all the other people sitting at that table were not the
direct descendants of Henrietta Lacks, the only person sitting there that was a direct descendant of Henrietta Lacks
was her oldest son, my dad Lawrence Lacks. To see our
own family members sit there with more concern for helping the same institutions that stole Henrietta's cells than
they have for their own family... it was a hard kick in the
gut. I was so disappointed to see how far that they had
divided this family. All I could think about was how my mom
and dad had been working to find out what was going on
with the HeLa cells since the early '70s, and every door was
shut in their face.

My father and I never agreed to the NIH deal. Even
when they had a second meeting, I went back to let them
know that my father said, "No deal!" But the NIH didn't
look at my father as a man, they followed the same pro-
tocol that was put in place hundreds of years ago—that
a black man's thoughts and opinions don't matter, even
when it comes to his own family. Same old bullshit. I felt as
if I had been thrown back into 1951. It felt like I was back in
the time even before Henrietta passed away, when they
decided to hide the fact that they had taken her cells... a
time when they openly stated that they didn't need permission from my grandfather. Now, in the year 2013, the
same thing was happening to my dad.

The foundation started by Rebecca Skloot has also created some tension in the years since the book's release. Shortly before the book came out, she started the Henrietta Lacks Foundation. It's supposed to be there to help my grandmother's descendants with medical expenses, scholarships, and other financial needs. Some of the contributions made by the foundation include a hearing aid for Abdul, some truck repairs for Sonny, and dental work for one of my nieces. I even got some dental work done. Now, don't get me wrong. These things are great, and I appreciate them, but it's still only a drop in the bucket compared to the money Rebecca Skloot made off of our family. And the process of getting help from the foundation is really degrading. We have to write in and pretty much beg Rebecca Skloot for help to do this and do that for the Lacks family.

It's hard for me to find the words to explain how the process made me feel. I had to fill out a form stating why I needed assistance and blah, blah, blah. It was so humiliating and frustrating that I ended up calling the foundation to ask them why we have to beg for help from her when she has profited so much from my family. Why do we have to send in papers to ask Rebecca Almighty for help? Why can't we have the compensation owed to us, so we can take care of our own medical and educational needs without having to ask her or the foundation for handouts? It makes us look and feel like helpless children. We have to get permission from Rebecca Skloot to better our lives. It's just humiliating.

Rebecca Skloot claims that some of her royalties were contributed to the foundation, along with some of the speaking fees, but I don't know if that's true. They are very secretive about what's in the foundation and how it's funded. They also had another website set up where people were donating money and it was a way for people to contact the family. Jeri was very secretive about what was in the account and how much money was in there, we ever saw any of it. My father requested the account password once, so he could see how much money was in there and who was trying to contact the family, but he was refused. In fact, as far as I know, Jeri was the only family member with the password. We had a family meeting to discuss the account and my father asked Jeri to share the password with him. She refused to give it to him, so we sat around the table discussing and arguing about it. Some other family members took Jeri's side at first, but once we explained our concerns about it even they told Jeri to give my dad the password. She still refused to give it to him though. She told us that the money was coming from public donations.

Here's a quote from Rebecca Skloot, where she talks about starting the foundation: "When I was working on the book, once I understood what the family had been through, I knew I didn't want to be someone who came along and benefited from the story without doing something for them in return. So, I started the Henrietta Lacks Foundation. The broader mission of the foundation is to provide assistance, grants for education, health care, and emergency needs for people who made significant contributions to science without their knowledge or consent and their descendants." She's constantly advertising how the money has been spent to help members of the family, which I think raises some privacy issues. She also claims that grants have been given to descendants of the Tuskegee Experiment, but I haven't ever seen any proof of that.

Our PR representative, Karen, put out a lot of inquiries and questions about the foundation's funding and payouts. When she and our lawyers started asking questions, Rebecca Skloot's lawyers came out blazing to defend her. They refused to give up any information about the fundraising of the expenditures, saying that they had to keep the donors and award recipients confidential. Yet, she is constantly advertising what the foundation has done for the Lacks family, including how much money family members have received and what they got the money for... so, where is our confidentiality? Then they tried to say that Rebecca Skloot tirelessly raises money for the foundation and works pro bono for it. Of course, she works pro bono. It would look bad if she was getting paid for it, and she's already made her millions, so she can afford to work pro bono. Again, she is made to look like the generous savior of the Lacks family, while we are made to look like helpless children.

Right after the book came out, my father, my wife, and I started a separate foundation in memory of my grandmother. We'd been able to raise some money for it and we were trying to get my dad to donate to various charities in the grandmother's name. Around this time, a letter came to my house. I have power of attorney over my dad, so I opened it up. It was from a man named Allen Wilks, saying that he was my dad's son and so forth and so on. At first, I thought I should put this in the trash, but I thought about it and decided to give it to my dad and let him make the decision about what to do with it. My dad met with him and began socializing with him, but I wasn't ready to meet him. Meanwhile, my wife and I were still finding causes for the foundation to support. My dad kept saying no to all of our suggestions though, and we were getting upset about it.

Then, one day out of the blue, my dad came and told us that he wanted to let Allen and his wife, Pam Wilks, take over the foundation. I was shocked and confused. I said, "What is wrong with you? You don't even know these people and you want to turn this over to him!" We went back and forth for some time until I finally just gave in. I called Allen on the phone and told him that I would give him control of the foundation under one condition... that he and his wife keep my dad's name on it. They agreed. My wife and I took our names off and put theirs on it.

A couple of months later, I found out that they let my dad take his name off of it. Allen never even called to tell me that my dad wanted his name off of it. He just did it. Now, my dad has no control over the Henrietta Lacks Foundation that we started. I have no idea why my father did that. It was just so strange, and I did not understand it at all. Allen may have been a nice guy, but this was right around the time when the Henrietta story was really out there, and I was skeptical of new people coming around. He's about a year or so younger than me and it makes me wonder why he waited until then to come forward. It hurts me that he never called to let me know about my dad wanting to take his name off of the foundation, and at this time my dad was starting to show signs of dementia and Alzheimer's. He seems to be all there, but he isn't always equipped to make rational decisions.

Jeri and other family members have started taking advantage of my dad's condition recently. They take him out to speaking events knowing that he would not be there if he was still in his right mind. I recently saw a picture from the 2019 Henrietta Lacks Symposium. They are parading my dad around, selfishly benefitting from his diminished memory. They had my dad out at this professional event in a sweater and some tennis shoes. My dad would have never gone out anywhere dressed like that. He always took pride in his appearance, especially when representing his mother and the family. I can look back at any photo or video of my dad attending meetings or giving interviews, and he was always sharply dressed.

I should also point out that my dad doesn't like confrontation, so he would sometimes say no to one person and yes to someone else. I would get frustrated with him because he would tell me one thing and tell other family members something completely different. I explained to my dad that I told Allen to leave his name on the foundation because I wanted to make sure that the immediate family wouldn't be cut out again. It took a lot for me to question my father's judgement. I always respected my father's thinking and his wishes, so it took me a while to realize that there was anything happening with my dad's thinking. Even my wife knew before I did. My dad was always the leader that I looked up to, and questioning his judgement was something I would never do.

The aftermath of this book has left a family deeply divided. Even before I was born, the siblings went to my mother and father for advice on how to do this or do that. They always showed them respect as the heads of the family... until Rebecca Skloot entered our lives. Her book took things to the point where the family stopped consulting with my parents on anything. Instead, they now turn to Jeri and Rebecca Skloot for guidance. They don't ask any other family members because they won't like what we have to say.

In the midst of it all, everything feels so untrustworthy now. Even with our own lawyers, it feels like they don't give us any understanding about what is happening or what route we should take from here. It's just frustrating and feels like a never-ending continuation. The Lacks family has been getting the screws to us ever since Johns Hopkins took my grandmother's cells. It's been an ongoing conspiracy against us—from the taking of the cells to hiding information, to changing Henrietta's name, to withholding medical information from the family but giving it to Rebecca Skloot.

It just goes on and on, from HBO to the pharmaceutical companies. It's just an illusion that Jeri and the others have control over anything. People are just throwing money their way to keep them happy, but it's not all about the money. It's about the control over your family's destiny.

Lawrence Lacks

My Family Photo

Mom and Dad – Christmas Kiss

LaDonna Johnson

9

A MEANINGFUL AFTERLIFE

t took awhile for me to really understand how important my grandmother's cells were to both medicine and
medical research.

I'd been hearing about the cells for years, but as I got
older, I wanted to learn as much as I could and to figure
some things out for myself. With my wife's help, we started
doing our own research on the internet, reading all kinds of
articles about the HeLa cells and what they've been used
for by scientists.

It's still crazy to think about how many of my grandmother's cells are out there. One article I read said that if
you laid them all out, end-to-end, they'd wrap around the
planet at least three times. Three times around the entire
planet... I can't even get my mind around it. That shows
how valuable Henrietta's cells have been and how much
they have actually been used over the past 60 years. With

my grandmother's cells, it was the first time in history that scientists were able to test vaccines, cures, and treatments on living human cells. From what I understand, before the HeLa cells, they had to use animal cells when doing these tests, which obviously wasn't a good substitution.

They call my grandmother immortal for a reason. Her cells just keep dividing and dividing. It's been more than six decades since her death and HeLa is still being used by doctors and scientists to help people all over the world.

When I decided to write this book, my wife and I went back through a bunch of the articles we had saved about the cells. There was so much stuff that I had forgotten about some of it. One of the articles we found reminded me of a documentary that I watched years ago, before the book or movie. It was called *The Way of the Flesh* and it was done by the BBC. I remember that they talked about how Henrietta's cells had been taken from her body and all the things they've been used for since. They said that Henrietta's cells have been duplicated so many times that, all together, they would weigh more than 400 times the weight of her body at her death.

That movie fascinated me. The things that they had done with my grandmother's cells were incredible. HeLa cells have been taken into space to study the effects of zero gravity on human flesh. How crazy is that? Those stars that I used to lay on the ground and gaze at on those summer nights in Clover... my grandmother's cells had been up in those stars—twice. In 1960 with the Soviet satellite and later inside the Discoverer XVIII satellite when it was sent to space. From my understanding, they found that the cells divided even faster in zero gravity. Since then, scientists have been using her cells to learn more about the effects of space travel on humans. That's some amazing stuff right there. This black woman from Clover, Virginia, is helping scientists get people into space.

The documentary also talked about how cosmetic companies have bought millions of Henrietta's cells to test beauty products for side effects. I find that funny because we've been told over and over that nobody is making any money from the sale of Henrietta's cells. Even the U.S. military used her cells. During the Cold War, they placed her cells next to atomic bomb tests to see how radiation would affect them. That is incredible to me. My grandmother's cells were actually used to test atomic bombs. It does make me wonder what else the military has done with HeLa though. They are much more secretive now, so we'll probably never know all the things they are doing with her cells.

Cancer studies were another use the documentary talked about. Apparently, scientists wanted to figure out whether cancer was an infectious disease, transferable through the environment. They took HeLa cells to a maximum-security prison in Ohio and injected them into volunteer prisoners. They put the cells right under the skin and monitored them to see if the cells would grow and cause cancer. Some of the prisoners did develop small tumors in the places where they injected the cells, but nobody got cancer. Henrietta's cells helped prove that cancer wasn't infectious.

The documentary also mentioned one of the biggest scientific breakthroughs from the HeLa cells... the cure for polio. But I learned more about that from our Tuskegee visit than I did from the film. When my wife and I were shown around the campus, they described how their scientists had been using the HeLa cells and how the school had played a role in bringing the polio cure to African American patients.

They explained to us that, before the vaccine, more than 10,000 people got polio every year. A doctor had developed a vaccine, but he needed to test it on a large scale to make sure it was safe. He had been using monkey cells, but they kept dying during the process, so the testing was costing a lot of money. When he found the HeLa cells, he got a cheaper way to conduct the tests because they could grow so quickly. Because of my grandmother's cells, a vaccine was developed and who knows how many lives were saved.

Tuskegee came into the picture when they mass-produced HeLa cells for use across the country in finding a polio vaccine. They recognized that the medical profession wasn't paying enough attention to the seriousness of polio in the black community. In fact, some white doctors tried to say that blacks were immune to polio, which wasn't true. In the 1930s, polio hit the South really hard, making both white and black kids sick. But the black children couldn't find good medical treatment, so many of them died from the disease. Seeing this problem, the school created the Tuskegee Infantile Paralysis Center to treat black children with polio, and to help black researchers fight against the disease.

With all of the lies and deceit around the taking and the use of my grandmother's cells, and how race has played a part in all of it, I was so happy to learn that my grandmother's cells had been used to help black children. I mean, it's a blessing that she has impacted people of all races all over the world, but it feels especially rewarding to know that she helped her own community as well, because she was always about helping her own.

I've also found articles about how Henrietta's cells were used in developing a cancer vaccine for girls. They found that the HeLa cells contained a strain of HPV that can lead to cervical cancer. The strain had entered her cells and disabled a gene that would have normally kept tumors from forming on her cervix. In the 1980s, scientists were able to use that information to create an HPV vaccine. From what I understand, the vaccine has helped to greatly reduce the number of HPV cases among teenage girls. Now, every time those HPV vaccine commercials come on television I can be proud that my grandmother helped to save young people from cancer.

My grandmother's cells also helped scientists create a technique called gene mapping. I think this is the reason they came and took blood from my father and his siblings.

Scientists use the technique to figure out the distance between genes on a cell. Then they can identify which genomes they want to study. In the 1960s, they combined HeLa cells with mouse cells, to create the first humananimal hybrid cells. They looked at the hybrid cells to develop their gene mapping techniques. This is the study that led to the NIH illegal partnership with the Lacks family. Some scientists published the results in a journal, putting our family DNA on display for everyone to see.

Without my grandmother's cells, the medical profession could not have taken the study and cure of viruses as far as it has gone. They have infected her cells with every virus from HIV, herpes, measles, and even Zika. Then, studied the cells to figure out ways to battle these viruses. HeLa cells are the most common cells used for HIV research. They helped scientists create a medicine cocktail that slows the disease down. Even today, my grandmother's cells are still being used in the areas of cloning, chemotherapy, and in vitro fertilization. They are the most used human cell lines in science over the last 60 years.

It's funny though, because the strength of my grandmother's cells has also given those scientists some headaches. In one article I read, researchers wanted to prove that even a small amount of radiation can lead to cancer. They took healthy human cells and exposed them to radiation. Then, they observed and measured the cell death to prove that low amounts of radiation can cause cancer. There was a problem though. The healthy cells they thought they were using had been infiltrated by my grandmother's malignant cells. In other words, HeLa had overgrown and contaminated the healthy cell lines. In fact, those strong HeLa cells have infiltrated cells all over the world. In the 1970s, five cell lines were transported from the Soviet Union to the United States. When they got here, researchers found that every one of those lines had been infected by HeLa. From what I've read, the cells can travel through air droplets and laboratory gloves. Some articles called the cells "laboratory weeds," because they grow so fast and contaminate any other cell lines present. I call them strong because they are Lacks family cells.

My grandmother's cells have been used to help so many people and to push science along to places we can't even imagine. I wish the circumstances had been different, and I hate that she was taken away from this world so young, but I'm proud of the legacy Henrietta left this world and the many lives that have been saved thanks to her cells.

Lawrence Lacks and Courtnee Lacks Brown

Right top: My great-grandmother Blanch Armstrong, left top: My grandmother Mildred Freedom, bottom left: Bobbette Lacks and LaDonna Johnson

My dad's boat

Lacks Family Meat Market

10

BACK TO WHY

After reading this book, I hope people will understand some important details. First, my grandmother was an amazing woman whose short life gave the world some of the most important medical discoveries of the last 60 years. Second, the Lacks family was a middle-class black family of people who worked hard and tried to build good lives for themselves. Third, our family has been torn apart and manipulated by Rebecca Skloot and her book *The Immortal Life of Henrietta Lacks*. Fourth, there was no NIH deal. Lastly, we have never seen, then or now, any compensation from the sale of my grandmother's cells or the sale of my grandmother's story. If I was able to communicate those five things, then I did what I set out to do with this book.

Despite what anyone might say, this book isn't about money or fame. It's all about the true story of Henrietta

Lacks and her family. Rebecca Skloot was the worst thing that could have ever happened to our family. People always say that without her, my grandmother's story would have never been told, but that's bullshit. Henrietta's story was starting to be told with or without Rebecca Skloot, and what good is the story being put out there if most of it is a lie? Her book is not about my grandmother. It was supposed to be about her, and Rebecca Skloot is constantly saying it's about her, but that book is really about Rebecca Skloot. When she sat in our backyard all those years ago and told my dad that this was her story, she was telling the truth. Because she made it her story. She used our name and our pain, then inserted herself to make herself rich and famous. Then, she left our family to deal with the aftermath of her lies and be satisfied with the crumbs she decides to give us every once in awhile.

The decision to write this book wasn't an easy one and it took a long time for me to make that decision. Starting off, it was because of how they portrayed my family, but then it was about how they cut my father out of everything that had to do with Henrietta. As more people became aware of her scientific contributions, they started having all of these ceremonies and recognitions for her, but my dad was cut out of all of it. They gave some events in Washington, D.C. and he wasn't invited. The White House ceremony... we weren't invited. I have a copy of the congressional honor where they went to D.C., but we were not invited to the ceremony. Just last year, we found out that a painting of Henrietta called "Henrietta Lacks (HeLa): The

Mother of Modern Medicine" had been unveiled at the Smithsonian National Portrait Gallery. We didn't know anything about it, and I think my dad would have loved to be there for that. There are so many examples. Not just the book, but how they treated him with such disrespect after the book.

My grandmother's contribution was amazing. Six scientists have won the Nobel Prize for the work they've done with HeLa cells. That's a big deal. Colleges and scientific organizations have named scholarships and programs for my grandmother. Even Johns Hopkins has finally recognized her. They have two Henrietta Lacks Symposiums every year, where they bring researchers together with the community to talk about how they can help everyday people. I read that more than 1,000 people attended the last one they held. Johns Hopkins also has an event for Baltimore high school students each year, which is called the Henrietta Lacks High School Symposium. The students get to spend the day at Johns Hopkins learning about biomedical research and bioethics. Then, there's the Henrietta Lacks East Baltimore Health Sciences Scholarship that gives a four-year scholarship of $10,000 per year to a graduate of Paul Laurence Dunbar High School. The Johns Hopkins Urban Health Institute also gives out the Henrietta Lacks Memorial Award of $15,000 for collaborations between the university and the community.

I love all of this, especially considering Johns Hopkins' poor reputation within the black community, but there is so much more that needs to be done. If I had my way, most of the money made from my grandmother's cells and story would go to help people within the community. There are so many people in Baltimore who need help. I have no doubt that my grandmother would want her legacy to include helping them. I'm not minimizing these programs, but when you look at how much money has been made off of my grandmother's cells, it just doesn't compare.

Our family has been told for years that nobody is profiting from the sale of my grandmother's cells, but that's an outright lie. Pharmaceutical companies are still lining their pockets with profits from HeLa. I read one article that talked about how cell banks and biotech companies sell vials of my grandmother's cells for about $260... and this article was dated. Who knows what a vial goes for now? I saw another report that said a vial can go for up to $1,000. Considering how many cells they sell every year, that's a ridiculous amount of money. But not one cent of that money goes to our family. Like I said before, a lot of people think we got royalties from book and movie sales, but we get nothing. It makes me so sad to think about how many people we could be helping with all of that money.

Whatever Henrietta's cells were making, I would give almost all of that money away to helping the needy and the poor. The real legacy of Henrietta Lacks is helping people. Yes, it's the American way to be fruitful, but you don't have to be greedy. A lot of what her cells are doing, I would like to give it back to small cities and urban areas, by teaching children entrepreneur skills and opening community centers. I want to help uplift members of the community in her name.

Then, there are the profits from the book. More than 1,000 colleges and universities require their students to read *The Immortal Life of Henrietta Lacks* every single year. Even high schools and scientific companies use it as required reading. That's a constant stream of profit going into Rebecca Skloot's pocket and thousands of students reading lies and negativity about the Lacks family every year. I don't know how much she actually made from book sales, but I know she made millions because it was a best seller for a long time. Even though we asked, nobody would ever tell us how much she made with the HBO deal either, because she sold the rights to Oprah. I think all of this secretiveness is on purpose, so the family won't know how much she actually made. It also helps her keep up the lie about helping the Lacks family. If people knew how much she actually made and compared it to any and all financial benefits received by the Lacks family because of the book, they would see that we got one drop from a great big pitcher of water.

Here's a quote from one letter we received from her lawyers: "In light of the support Ms. Skloot and the Foundation has provided to your clients and their family, Lawrence Sr.'s, Lawrence Jr.'s, Ron's... ingratitude is deeply troubling." They talk like we are supposed to grovel at her feet with gratitude, but what are we supposed to be thankful for. The division she caused within our family? Maybe the lies she told about us? Are we supposed to be thanking her for making millions off of our family story and providing us with some sporadic healthcare that we have to beg her to receive? I would really like to know why our strong black family is supposed to show gratitude to this conniving woman.

I know some people will read this book and still say that I am all about the money, but the money is only part of it… and why shouldn't I be concerned about creating wealth for my family. Even for Jeri and all of them that signed their rights away. We may be on separate sides of this, but we are still family and I want to see all of us rise together. I want to create generational wealth for our children and grand-children, and what's wrong with that? My grandmother would want to see all of us rise. I guarantee that before it's all over, those pharmaceutical companies are going to profit more and more from Henrietta's cells, and all I want to do is make sure my family is taken care of in all of this. It's the American dream to always get ahead, yet I'm wrong for asking questions about the money? I'm not the one out here selling my grandmother's parts. They are.

Even Oprah talked about the compensation we should have received. She said, "The fact that they were never compensated for any of those cells by any of the drug companies, that is really unfortunate. I do think they should have been compensated by somebody who prof-ited from it."

Though we've had more lawyers than we can count, no lawsuits have been filed on our behalf. We've been given every response you can imagine. Some of them said the statute of limitations has passed on any cause of action we may have had. Some of them said that we can't sue because Johns Hopkins had a legal right to take our grandmother's cells without permission. We were also told that my grandmother's name and likeness became public domain after her death, so we can't sue anyone for using them to make money. Even our efforts to claim the cells as part of my grandmother's estate were turned down. I mean you name an excuse not to sue, and we have heard it multiple times. Meanwhile, these pharmaceutical companies are still out here making money off of HeLa every single day. I so proud of what Henrietta's cells were able to accomplish, but you have to stop the greed behind it. I would rather give them away for free than to have these drug company executives out here creating generational wealth for their families off of them.

Let me be clear about something though. I'm doing fine. My bills are paid, and my family can eat well every single day. It's the future Lacks generations that I am thinking about and making sure that they get a fair start in life. The pharmaceutical executives' children will be rich and well off from Henrietta's cells, but my family has to struggle because of it? It's not right. The money part of it... the Lacks family has gone this long without it and we don't really think anything is going to come of it. In fact, I doubt that the family will ever see justice in my lifetime, but that's not all that this book is about.

The family closeness is gone now. Our relationships are completely different now. The cousins I grew up with barely even speak to me anymore. We all used to gather in my mother's backyard all the time, but there haven't been any gatherings like that since the book came out. I mean, I know families grow up and grow apart, but this is more than that. Even when time and distance separates family, they still get together once in a while to catch up and connect... but we don't even do that. The strain of the book and the division of it had a lot to do with the family separation.

All of this tension really took its toll on me. It took awhile for me to realize it, but I started to feel sad and depressed. This entire situation tore me down to the point where I was constantly angry and sad. While all of this was going on, I was also caring for my mother after her stroke, which further compounded my feelings during this time. My hands were tied about how much I could do because I had to be available 24/7 for my mom. I knew the situation was bothering me and that I needed to do something more, but I had no idea what to do; and even if I did, there was no time to actually do it.

Though I was feeling really bad, I never thought about getting any kind of professional help. I don't have too much trust for doctors anymore. They just want to put you on a bunch of unnecessary drugs with all of these crazy side effects. I think back to all of the medications they had my mother on for years. I don't want to go as far as calling them legalized drug dealers, but you are always hearing about unnecessary prescriptions and surgeries. I am more about natural cures. Your body is your main source for healing yourself if you take care of it properly. I mean, you can't live without doctors, but you've got to weigh the cost of dealing with one, and you have to ask questions. I decided to work on myself instead of seeking help from a doctor.

What helped to bring me out of my depression was sitting and talking with my mom, letting her know what's going on. She always stood up for the family and did what she had to do. I soon realized it fell on me to make sure that my family's true story was told. My mom is incapacitated, my dad is going down, my Uncle Sonny isn't well... all the people who were the strength of the family are no longer. So, I have to straighten up and fly right. I took all of that anger and finally decided to do something about it. I always felt like family was everything, but I had to realize that not everyone feels that way. I came out of that depression and felt much better about the situation, knowing that it wasn't because of me or my dad that the family is so divided now.

I took a different look at it and decided that the real story needed to come out. Day has passed on. He lived a good life in his later years. He was always such a lovable person, period. He was a little player after Henrietta died, but then he found a good woman to settle down with. I thank God for Ms. Marjorie Lacks. She took good care of my grandfather at the end. He wanted to leave her with something, so they married, and he lived with her until the day he died. They were together for a good twenty years. In one transcript of the book, Rebecca Skloot tried to say that Day died alone in the hospital. She had to take it out of the final book though because it was a bold face lie.

My Uncle Sonny had a stroke some years back. I am convinced that this whole book situation took its toll on him. He was like a hero to me, but he can't speak for himself anymore. Knowing my uncle though, he wouldn't be happy with the route that the family has taken. Around the time when he had his stroke, they were marching him all around to those speaking engagements. He was flying here and flying there, and you could tell it was taking a toll on him. I remember one time, they brought Sonny to my house. When we went to the door to greet him, we looked at his face and immediately said, "Take that man to the hospital. Something's not right!" In fact, we noticed it twice. Once at the house and once at a Science Center event. Even another cousin noticed that something was wrong with him. It wasn't good at all and shortly after that, he had a stroke.

Sonny was in denial about the book for such a long time. He wanted monetary value for the family, which was totally understandable. He would often tell my father, "Look, let's just try to get something." It wasn't until later that he realized what kind of mistake he made. At one time, he started trying to talk positive about the family and saying the family was educated, but they told him they could sue him for talking about something not in the book... all because he had signed his rights away. I remember when he tried to say that Henrietta could read and write, they took him in the office and told him he could not do that. After that, you could see the joy fade out of him. I think that's what led to Sonny's stroke. You could see everything was bothering him.

Even with their differences over the book, my dad and Sonny always remained close. After all, my dad practically raised Sonny and he did for him just like he did for his own kids. Sonny was a truck driver too, and my dad bought him a tractor-trailer to drive. He was always there for Sonny and his family when they needed him. I was really close with Sonny's three children growing up, but we hardly talk at all anymore. Before my dad's health started to decline, he would go to both of his brothers' homes to visit and make sure they were all right. He was still trying to be the head of the family, but he is getting too old. I told him that it was time to let someone else step up and do some things. This whole thing has really worn him down. The type of person he was, regardless of who did sign the contract and who didn't sign the contract, he still wanted to help everybody. But to see his family so torn, it truly breaks his heart.

He also still worries that his mother isn't truly at rest. He thinks that with the constant use of her cells, her soul will never truly be at rest from the spiritual side of things. I read an article that said you could take Henrietta's cells and fill the empire state building two or three times. That's how many cells they made of hers. That has to have a spiritual impact. My dad could be right in thinking that she will never be at rest and she definitely can't rest knowing that her family is divided like it is.

My dad was totally torn between doing the right thing and being with the other side of the family. While he took care of everybody, my mother handled the hammer making sure everything went the way it was supposed to... and he lost that when my mother had her stroke. Like I said before, my dad didn't always treat my mom the way he should have, but no matter how strained their relationship became, my mother always had the Lacks family legacy at heart. I could see the pain on my mother's face when we would talk about the book, and my father's frustration with the way they belittled his family. After all, my father's siblings weren't like siblings. They were like his children that he and mom helped to raise and loved unconditionally.

I'm still nervous about putting this book out there, but my love for my family and our legacy is bigger than my fear. I actually hate to hear myself speak. There is just something about it that scares me. I remember after I did my first radio show interview, everyone wanted to sit back and listen to it, but I was too afraid to listen with other people. My wife couldn't understand why, and to tell the truth, I couldn't either. I just went into the other room because I was fearful of hearing myself say something stupid. So, doing this book is a big step for me. But after seeing all these people out there with their own personal agendas—none of them wanting to tell the truth about the Lacks family—I knew I had to speak out.

I try to speak truth to power. This book is about speaking the truth about the power of Henrietta Lacks and the legacy she left behind in the Lacks family. I don't know what will come out of this. I hope it sparks a conversation about inaccuracies and the portrayal of our family in Rebecca Skloot's book. I also hope it will force my family to communicate with one another, so we can resolve our differences and move on together. But more than anything, I hope people will learn the truth about Henrietta Lacks and the beautiful legacy that she and my grandfather left behind. Not only the immortal cells, but also that some of her family are as tough as she was and that we are her voice. I'm so grateful that my father, Lawrence Lacks, is still here to tell her story, because it's very rare that you can actually write about the history of someone and hear it directly from someone that was there.

I am proud to be the oldest grandson of Henrietta Lacks and I will always stand up to protect the elders of my family.

* * *

Learn more about Henrietta Lacks and her story online at www.henriettalacksuntold.com.

My Grandchildren Ja'Shawn Barber and Vera Williams

My Pack – Babie, Bear, Rock, and Woodie

Ron Lacks and Ella Williams

My Wife – Hope Lacks

145

Schoolhouse in Clover Virginia

These are the things that Henrietta Lacks said to her son Lawrence Lacks before she passed away...

*I've enjoyed each and every precious moment
spent here on earth, raising a family*

*There's no greater pleasure than watching
your love one's blossom*

I don't worry that I'll ever be forgotten

Knowing how you were raised

We prepared you for these on coming days

My soul will be at rest knowing I gave you my best

Henrietta Lacks

Henrietta's signature, giving her blessing

146